Dealing with D

Other maths publications by Steve Chinn

'Mathematics for Dyslexics: A Teaching Handbook' 3rd edition
(2007) Chinn, SJ and Ashcroft, JR, published by Wiley

'The Trouble with Maths' (2004) Steve Chinn, published by
RoutledgeFalmer.
(Winner of the NASEN/Times Educational Supplement
'Book for Learning and Teaching Award' 2004)

'What to do when you can't learn the times tables' (1996)
Chinn, SJ, published by Egon

'What to do when you can't add and subtract' (1998)
Chinn, SJ, to be published by Egon

'What to do when you can't learn the times tables' on CD-ROM.
Available from iANSYST www.iansyst.com or Ann Arbor
www.annarbor.co.uk

'Dyslexia and Numeracy' Chapter 5 in 'Adult Dyslexia:
A Guide for Learndirect Tutors and Support Staff' ADO/ufi

Website www.stevechinn.co.uk

Dealing with Dyscalculia

Sum Hope²

STEVE CHINN

SOUVENIR PRESS

First published in 2007 by Souvenir Press Ltd,
43 Great Russell Street, London WC1B 3PD

Portions of this book appeared in slightly different
form in *Sum Hope* (Souvenir Press).

ISBN 9780285637986

Typeset by M Rules

Printed and bound in Great Britain

Contents

Introduction

Getting Started

People make maths difficult. Those 'people' may be teachers, parents, children, education policy makers, even mathematicians. Those books that offer to make everyone a maths genius only make it easy for the first few pages. In fact by having lots of pages those books can't be making it that easy, and certainly not quick.

If you work with the ideas in this book, then everyday maths will become much easier. Like any new skill, you will need to practise and keep in trim by refreshing that skill every once in a while, but I have taken the subject and minimised the skill and memory loads so that the task is manageable.

Most people have a comfort zone for maths, an area where they feel relatively comfortable. It may not be a big zone, but it will be the place to start new learning. What this book will try to do is to show you how the knowledge and skills you already have, however small, can be extended to many more skills and knowledge of maths.

And, if you start to feel confident and want to go on to higher skill levels, the strategies set out in this book will have given you the sound foundations you need to pursue that goal.

1 Why Some People Find it Hard to Learn Maths

Some people are good at tennis, some are good at writing stories, others are good at maths. What makes someone good or bad at something will be a mixture of things, and just how good, or how bad you are will depend on a combination of the strengths of each of those things and how hard you work at the skill.

Maths is no different to any other skill. There are people who are natural mathematicians and people for whom numbers create a total blackout. Then there are lots in between. Just how good these 'in-between' people are will depend on their experiences as they try to learn maths.

It will depend on how well they are taught and whether that teaching meets their learning needs and their learning style. It will also depend on what pre-requisite sub-skills they bring to the processes of learning maths.

Even that is not the whole story, because the success will also depend on motivation and the ability to find alternative learning solutions for the times when the first solution does not work (for you).

However, you may have reached the stage where you have decided that enough is enough and that you and mathematics can live without each other. I hope to persuade you to have one more try. It is such a useful skill for so many aspects of life.

When you have any sort of problem, a good starting point is to try and understand the causes of the problem. This often helps you understand the problem itself and should make it easier to tackle. This awareness may even help you to avoid or at least reduce the influence of these problems in the future.

So, if you can't do mathematics it is likely to be for some very good reasons, which probably have little to do with how clever you are.

There are many factors that can get in the way of learning mathematics. I will explain some of these factors in this chapter. You may recognise some of them as relevant to you. You may be unlucky enough to be affected by all of them, but even then you may have found ways to get round some or most of the difficulties these factors create. If you haven't, this book will help you to find some ways.

So, let's look at these problem factors ...

Anxiety

Anxiety can really get in the way of learning. In fact it can be a total barrier to learning.

It is an accumulation, a consequence of all the other factors and difficulties and how they have affected your attempts to succeed in mathematics, and how they have affected your attitude towards wanting to carry on working at this subject.

Anxiety is the last difficulty to occur, because it is a consequence of all the other problems and it is the first you have to overcome if you are to return to using mathematics and numbers. Even though it is the last difficulty, the seeds may have been sown when you were quite young. Sadly, once it is there, future experiences tend to strengthen that state. Anxiety can become a self-perpetuating experience.

So, although it is the last difficulty to occur, it will probably be the first one we have to overcome.

One of the best ways to reduce your anxiety is to find some areas where you can succeed. It is important for you to know that everyone can do some maths. As my colleague, Richard Ashcroft says, mathematics is a subject that builds like a wall, but it is a wall that can still stand and be strong with some gaps, some missing bricks.

You do not have to be perfect, or even good in every bit of maths to be a successful mathematician.

For example, an ex-student of mine still cannot give an instant answer to 'What is 8×7?' This lack of knowledge might cause some people to be anxious, but Jake does now have a degree and that degree is in maths. As he said when we last met, they don't ask you 'What is 8×7 in the third year of a maths degree.'

And, if it is mistakes that make you anxious, trust me, even good mathematicians make mistakes in maths.

The work in this book will attempt to use and build on what you know, because that makes sense as an approach. It is amazing how a little maths knowledge can be made to go a long way, especially if it is a truly useful and good little bit of knowledge.

To be good, or even just OK at mathematics you have to practise, but if you are anxious about maths you will probably try to avoid doing any practise at all! For you to feel more comfortable and then, hopefully, confident I have to convince you to change your mind and try some maths.

If you do suffer from maths anxiety you are certainly not alone. There have been whole books written on this subject. My guess is that people who are mathematically anxious are in the majority!

How I feel about Maths. A Questionnaire

The twenty items below are about maths and your feelings when you have to do each one of these things. Read and consider to each item and then decide how anxious that situation makes you feel. If it **never** makes you feel anxious write 1 in the space, if it makes you feel anxious **sometimes** write 2, if it makes you feel anxious **often** write 3 and if it **always** makes you feel anxious write 4.

1 = never anxious **2** = sometimes anxious **3** = often anxious
4 = always anxious

1 Working out the tip for the waiter in a restaurant. ____
2 Working out the prices of things when you
   are abroad. ____
3 Checking the cost of your shopping. ____
4 Working out 20% off in a sale. ____
5 Checking your change when shopping. ____
6 Working out the cost of a holiday. ____
7 Adding the four prices ... £5.99 + £10.99 + £19.99
   + £3.95 on a mail order form. ____
8 Reading a train timetable. ____
9 Working out your weekly budget. ____
10 Checking which mobile phone deal is the best value. ____
11 Converting your weight in stones to kilograms. ____
12 Having to recall a maths fact quickly (such as 6×9). ____
13 Understanding the odds for a bet on the
    Grand National. ____
14 Writing a cheque. ____
15 Checking the VAT amount on a Builder's
    bill/invoice. ____
16 Working out your pay rise when you are told it will
    be 3.25%. ____
17 Checking your credit card bill. ____
18 Working out how much weedkiller you need to
    use in a 5 litre sprayer. ____
19 Changing the quantities in a recipe for 4 when
    cooking for 6 people. ____
20 Remembering your maths lessons at school. ____

Add up your total score (OK, I know that is doing
some maths!)

Look at page 7 to learn more about your score TOTAL _____

Do try the ideas in this book. They are designed to help you succeed and to start to overcome that anxiety.

Learning how to do maths successfully will help reduce anxiety. Set your own targets and your own speed of working. Make both of these realistic, and then slowly increase your goals. Above all ... **begin the journey**.

From my initial results on this on-going survey the average score was 34. A score of 60 and above would suggest that you are in the top 3.5% for anxiety levels. The top eight anxiety items, in order, were: stones to kilograms, Grand National, memories of maths at school, 3.25% pay rise, money abroad, VAT on the builder's bill, mobile phone deals and weedkiller. Writing a cheque created the least anxiety.

Memory

Any subject or area of study will have a body of knowledge that you will need to know. You may not need to remember it all, all of the time. For example, if you cannot bring a particular word to mind in a conversation where you are trying to speak in French, it may be that you can find a suitable alternative. The same is true of maths. You will need to remember quite a lot of facts and procedures, but you may well be able to find alternative strategies for the times when your memory fails you.

One of the greatest supports for maths memory is to understand maths.

Howard Gardner taught us about multiple intelligences, for example we may have a musical intelligence or an intra-personal intelligence. He also says that we may not have all these intelligences at the same level. You may be a gifted linguist, but a hopeless mathematician. You may be a superb sportsman, but a terrible musician. I think the same is true for memory. You may have a truly wonderful memory for foreign languages, but be unable to remember a phone number, but to be good at maths you need a good mathematical memory or efficient ways of using and extending the memory you do have. This mathematical memory can be for facts and procedures. We call this 'long term memory'. There is also the memory that holds information for a short while why we carry out a calculation. This is 'short term memory'. Some people can hold seven or eight items in their short term memory, for example an eight digit phone number. Some can hold only two or three items. Obviously this will have a serious effect on their ability to do any maths mentally.

One of the most commonly occurring problems in mathematics is remembering and retrieving from long term memory the basic facts for numbers, in particular the times (or multiplication) table facts such as 6×7 and 4×9. Some people find the task of memorising all these facts virtually impossible. And since this is one of the first demands from teachers of mathematics it can create an early sense of failure and inadequacy.

You do not need to remember ALL of these multiplication facts, just the KEY ones (see Chapter 4).

If someone asks you to recall a fact from memory, say a times table fact, and your memory is a blank, it is something like looking into a deep black pit. There seems to be no way out and if remembering the fact is your only option, then indeed, there is no way out. I will try to provide some strategies to stop you falling into that pit.

Mathematical memory can also let you down when learning addition and subtraction facts, such as $7 + 8$ and $13 - 6$, but often these facts can be accessed just by counting, often quite quickly, on your fingers. The times table and addition facts are the basic building blocks of number work, but if you cannot remember them, all is not lost, there are some ideas to help (see Chapter 4). Many of the ideas in this book try to pull together and interrelate the number facts and methods, so that they become mutually supportive. The idea is that you practise and learn fewer facts, so consequently you practise these key facts more often as you use them to access other facts.

Your mathematical memory may also let you down when you try to recall a procedure or method, such as how to work out percentages. I will try to make each new process real by relating it to something you know in 'real' life and then relate it to something mathematical that you already know. The goal is to create a good understanding of each topic as you develop your own meaning for maths.

A complex mental arithmetic task may overload your short term memory and cause a total breakdown in the process you are trying to perform so I have included some suggestions to reduce the possibility of this problem occurring and help you improve your mental arithmetic.

Despite what many people think, there are often alternative methods for doing maths. Some of us were taught by teachers who insisted that we 'Do it this way.' Some of the methods for doing arithmetic are best when written, some are better adapted to use 'in your head'. One of the reasons for short term memory overload is that people often try to use written methods for mental arithmetic. Not all written methods transfer successfully to mental arithmetic, because they tend to have too many steps. I will attempt to suggest which are the methods that are better to use for each case.

Any memory decays or slips away. What keeps it in your mind are frequent reminders. The more you see, hear, say or feel (putting a memory into the brain by all senses) a particular experience, the more securely it will be fixed in your mind.

Words

Sometimes the words people use when talking about arithmetic are confusing. I have a similar problem when a fluent computer expert starts explaining new software to me. It seems to me that they have a language of their own (which, of course, they do!)

One source of possible confusion in our early experience of maths is that we use more than one word for a particular mathematics meaning, for example, adding can be … 6 *more than* 3, 17 *and* 26, 52 *plus* 39, 15 *add* 8

Sometimes the words we use have other, non-mathematical

meanings, for example 30 *take away* 12, 18 *shared between* 3 people.

Sometimes the same words can mean two things, for example; 'What is 5 more than 8?' is addition, 5 + 8, but 'Emily has 16 sweets. She has 6 more than Sarah. How many sweets does Sarah have?' This is subtraction, 16 – 6. Word problems are a major difficulty for children worldwide and I am sure they have contributed to the anxiety and reluctance of many adults to do maths.

Sometimes the words we use for the more common everyday examples of mathematics ideas do not fit the normal pattern of other words we use in that topic. For example with fractions we have special names for the two most common values, $\frac{1}{2}$ is called one half and $\frac{1}{4}$ is called one quarter rather than one second and one fourth (which would fit better into the pattern we use for other fractions such as one sixth, one seventh, one eighth, one ninth). Clear patterns with no exceptions to the rule help memory to be effective. Sadly maths does not always oblige.

The teen numbers are another case of a break with the main pattern and they can cause possible confusion, especially for young children when they meet two digit numbers (11, 12, 13, 14, 15, 16, 17, 18, 19) for the first time. The way we say the teen numbers is backwards to numbers in the twenties, thirties, forties and other two digit numbers. So we say eighteen (eight ten) and write 18, then we say twenty eight, which has the digits in the correct word order 28. This particular situation is exacerbated by the words eleven (which could be oneteen, or better, one ten and one) and twelve (which could be twoteen or one ten and two) and hindered by the teen numbers such as thirteen (threeteen) and fifteen (fiveteen). I suppose a small real life benefit of eleven and twelve is that they save two more teenage years.

Although these examples may sound simple, they can be enough to start an impression in the learner that maths is confusing and inconsistent. Early maths is frequently inconsistent which does not help learners who are looking for patterns and the security that those patterns offer.

Sequences and patterns

Sequences and patterns such as 2, 4, 6, 8, 10, 12 … or 10, 20, 30, 40, 50, 60 … are very much a part of maths. You need to be able to remember them and often adapt them. So 10, 20, 30, 40 … can be adapted to 13, 23, 33, 43, 53 … Some people find this adaptation difficult. The odd numbers pattern (1, 3, 5, 7, 9, 11 …) is far less familiar than the even numbers pattern (2, 4, 6, 8, 10, 12 …)

If you can remember and recognise sequences and patterns it will help your memory. For example it is much easier to remember the seven numbers 1234567 than a random set such as 5274318. Sometimes it helps if the digits or the numbers are chunked in twos or threes.

Speed

Not only do people expect you to do maths correctly, they often expect you to do it quickly. Trying to work more quickly than you naturally would do will increase the pressure on you and will almost certainly make you less accurate. This is like taking up jogging. You cannot convert yourself from a couch potato to a 5 minute mile runner overnight (and you may never ever reach that 5 minute goal, nor want to!). If you do want to start jogging, or squash, or oil painting or fishing you will need to learn new skills and practise them and build up the skill over a period of time.

As you practise you get faster and the task gets easier, or to be precise, because the task stays the same, you find the task easier. Then you can try to add in more skills and thus become more sophisticated in performing the tasks. When you can make a skill or a memory automatised then it will make less demands on your short term and working memories and there is more memory to do harder tasks. Automatisation usually requires lots of practise and confidence in the task.

Thinking Style

It seems obvious to say that not everyone thinks the same way. We have our own thinking style for all the different things we do in life and this includes having our own thinking style for maths.

Our thinking style (or cognitive style if you want to sound psychological) is the way we work out maths problems. It is very much a characteristic of each individual, but it is possible to simplify the range of thinking styles down a little and imagine that our own thinking style lies somewhere along a line or a spectrum. At one end of this spectrum are the *inchworms* and at the other end are the *grasshoppers*.

An inchworm likes to work with formulas and fixed methods. Inchworms work step by step, preferring to write things down. They see the details of a problem.

They also tend to see numbers exactly as they are written, a sort of numerical equivalent of a literal interpretation. This can be a disadvantage if you have a limited number of facts ready for retrieval from memory.

A grasshopper often goes straight to an answer. They have a really good sense of numbers and how we manipulate them in maths. Grasshoppers rarely write down any 'working'. They like to see the whole picture – they overview. They are intuitive and can be confused by formulas (or see no reason to use them). They tend to see a broad value in numbers, inter-relating them to comfortable values, for example 97 is seen as a 'bit less than' 100 or 25 is seen as half and then half again of 100.

If someone tries to explain a grasshopper method to an inchworm, the inchworm learner will probably not relate to the method. And vice-versa. This could be one cause of failure to understand maths. An inchworm teacher may not be able to communicate effectively with a grasshopper student and a grasshopper teacher may not provide explanations and methods that an inchworm learner can understand.

For example, an inchworm will add 340 and 97 step by step, starting with the units, that is the 0 add 7, then they move to the tens and add 4 and 9 and finally the hundreds and add the carried

1 to the 3 to give an answer of 437. Inchworm thinkers usually like to use pen and paper to write down their method, probably as

$$\begin{array}{r} 340 \\ + 97 \\ \hline 437 \end{array}$$

Faced with the same question, a grasshopper will look at the 97 and round it up to 100, add 340 and 100 and subtract the 3 (which made 97 into 100), getting an answer of 437 without writing anything down.

> **It is best if you can learn how to make use of both thinking styles. Generally speaking, grasshoppers are better at mental arithmetic and estimating, while inchworms are good at using formulas and detailed work. So you can see that to be versatile in your maths skills you need to be able to draw on both styles of thinking.**

Some people are set at the extremes of the style spectrum and find it very hard to adjust to the other style.

If you are an extreme inchworm and your memory for number facts and procedures is poor then you are likely to show many of the characteristics of a dyscalculic.

If you are an extreme grasshopper and you are also very impulsive and prone to mistakes then you too may present as a dyscalculic. (A serious downside of mistakes is that they are often better remembered than the correct stuff).

Inchworm	Grasshopper
Looks at the parts. Separates the problem into parts. Tends to start without overviewing	Looks at the whole. Overviews the whole problem
Tries to find the right formula or procedure to use	Focuses on finding a good estimate
Takes the numbers as they are given	Adjusts or combines the numbers to make the calculation easier

Works step by (little) step. No pre-estimate of what the answer may be.	Heads straight for the answer. Often works back from a trial answer
Focused on method	Focused on numbers
Much more secure if able to write, even if just tallies	Tends to do all the calculation mentally and finds it hard to explain/document how they worked out the answer
Often has no way of evaluating their answer	Appraises their answer. Checks by another method

Throughout this book you will see that some methods are more inchworm friendly and some are more grasshopper friendly. It may well be your thinking style that makes some methods easier to understand than others.

This means that there is no universal way to learn maths. A method that works for some may not work for others. The Inchworm and Grasshopper theory is a good illustration of why this is so.

Remember, both thinking styles have strengths and weaknesses. You need to learn the best of both.

Learning and teaching is about effective communication. For example, an inchworm style teacher may not find it easy to communicate ideas to a grasshopper learner. An inchworm learner may not be able to explain their methods to a grasshopper teacher.

If you want to check your thinking style, do the 'Thinking Style Test' in Appendix 3 at the end of this book.

Attitude

This is closely linked to anxiety and is a good final topic for this chapter.

One of the attitudes adopted by people who are not succeeding in maths is the attitude of not caring, not trying. This is usually based on the idea of protecting yourself from being wrong, from failing. Failure is something that any sensible person tries to avoid. So if you do not try to answer a question you cannot get it wrong. But this also means that by not allowing yourself to be wrong you are not allowing yourself to learn. I hope to encourage you to take the risk of sometimes being wrong.

One of the key factors for success is a willingness to take a risk. If you look at every number problem and think to yourself, 'I can't even begin that' then you will not learn. You need to practise and experience new ideas.

Often in schools children are placed in situations where they are asked a question to which they do not know the answer. Rather than be wrong, they do not try. They are withdrawing from a learning opportunity ... understandably.

So ...

You have to be involved in the process of learning maths. Learning is not a 'sit back and hope for something to happen' activity. This book will help you learn some new ways to do maths, but only if you practise the ideas. I wish I could provide a magic learning pill which you could take each day to give you instant knowledge and understanding, but I can't. The magic only comes from a combination of (hopefully) good explanations by the teacher and a willingness by the learner to practise and take risks.

2   Understanding Numbers and How to Write Cheques

When we write numbers they are made up by different combinations of just ten symbols / digits.

These ten symbols / digits are:

1, 2, 3, 4, 5, 6, 7, 8, 9, and 0

Our number system is based on groups of tens. It is no coincidence that we have ten fingers!

To explain how written numbers are built up I have used an example which shows how you count to, and write, one hundred and eleven as 111.

Imagine you have a job as a sheep counter and that you are counting a large number of sheep (and still staying awake). You can count up to the first nine sheep by using your fingers and writing the numbers with one number symbol / figure, for example 6. When you get to ten you can start again counting the next ten sheep on your fingers, but you call in a second sheep counter to record that you have one ten already counted. You ask your second sheep counter to use one finger to represent the one ten you have just counted. This is bringing in a second number symbol / figure. Let's say you have counted sixteen sheep, then you can use two of the number symbols / figures to write this down as ...

1 6

(for the first ten you counted)   (for the next 6 you counted)

We can use some or all of the ten number symbols written together (in an order which also tells us about the value of the number) to represent any number of sheep. For example forty five sheep is written as …

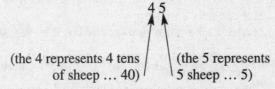

(the 4 represents 4 tens of sheep … 40)   (the 5 represents 5 sheep … 5)

So the first 4 you write represents 4 groups of ten (40) and the second digit, the 5, represents 5 units or 5 single sheep (5)

Imagine now that you have counted ninetynine sheep. Your second sheep counter has used nine fingers for his counting and you also have nine fingers counted. This is written down as

$$9\ 9$$

(for the nine tens the second sheep counter has counted)   (for the nine sheep you have counted)

The first 9 you write represents 9 tens (90) and the second 9 represents 9 units (9).

Now, think what happens to the counting when the next sheep after number 99 appears. You reach another ten on your fingers and the second sheep counter also reaches ten fingers (but, remember that his fingers are representing ten groups of ten).

You now need to bring in a third sheep counter to count one finger which will represent 1 hundred which is the word we use for ten lots of ten.

The number one hundred, is written in digits as 100. Now we are using three symbols or digits, 1 and 0 and 0. The third sheep counter's fingers count the hundreds, which are ten lots of ten.

The next sheep takes us to 101, so the second sheep counter still has zero tens to count. However, you need him there or you might think there are only 11 sheep,

Another ten sheep take us to one hundred and eleven sheep 111.

You are the units counter and you have one finger counted to represent 1 sheep.

The second sheep counter is the tens counter and he has one finger counted to represent 1 lot of ten sheep.

The third sheep counter is the hundreds counter and he has one finger counted to represent 1 group of hundred sheep.

So in 111, each 1 represents a different value.

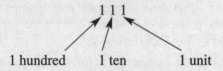

You have used three digits/symbols to represent the number one hundred and eleven. In this particular number all three digits are 1, but each 1 represents a different amount … 1 hundred, 1 ten and 1 unit.

This is the way all numbers are built up and written. So, when you get to *thousands* you bring in a fourth symbol / digit, so, for example five thousand, six hundred and eighty nine is:

5 689

The way the position of a digit in a number controls its value is called 'place value'.

It means that the place a digit takes in a number tells us its value.

The place tells us if the digit is a unit, a ten, a hundred, a thousand and so on

Note that when I wrote 5 689, the thousands digit was written with a gap between the thousands digit and the hundreds digit. This is a convention designed to help you visually organise the digits in a large number. Sometimes we use a comma 5,689.

The next place value takes us to five symbols, for example:

23 467

This takes us up to *ten thousands*.

We read 23 467 as:

twenty three thousand, four hundred and sixty seven

Then we go to six digit numbers, for example; **9**54 781

This takes us to *hundred thousands*.

We read 954 781 as:

nine hundred and fifty four thousand, seven hundred and eighty one

When we reach a thousand thousands, a seven digit number, we introduce a new name: a *million*.

One million is: 1 000 000

We read **3** 256 942 as:

three million, two hundred and fifty six thousand, nine hundred and forty two.

Our next new name for a number will be a *billion* and this will occur when we reach a thousand million: 1 000 000 000.

So, to go back over place value again, what mathematicians mean is that the value of a particular digit in a number depends on its place (or position) within that number. So, in the number

3 256 942

there are two 2's. The 2 between the 3 and the 5 represents 200 000, two hundred thousand and the 2 at the right hand end represents just 2, two units. So the place value of the same digit can make its value very different!

The most common problem with writing a number in digits from a number in words occurs when there are zeros in the number. In the million number example above (3 256 942) there was a digit for every place value. Look back at page 18 and the number one hundred and one. There are only two number words but you need three digits to write the number 101. The zero is needed to show that the number is more than 100. Without the zero the number is 11.

Try a slightly harder example ... four thousand and sixty five ... 4065.

There are three word digits (four, sixty and five), but it is a four digit number. The zero is used because there are zero (no) hundreds. Without the zero, the number becomes four hundred and sixty five: 465.

Go harder again ... five hundred thousand and six ... 500 006. There are two word digits (five and six) for a six figure number. Without the zeros this big number becomes 56!

How to write word numbers in digits (useful for cheques)

Businesses often have special cheques for big sums of money (where mistakes can be expensive).

This gives a good strategy for writing numbers as figures. Work to a place value grid:

million	hundred thousand	ten thousand	thousand	hundred	ten	unit

Take the number and read it, for example:

seven million, four thousand and ten
(just in case you win the Lottery)

Mark College

Date _____

BARCLAYS BANK PLC
BARCLAYS BUSINESS CENTRE
NEW BRANCH
P.O. BOX A, 1 HIGH STREET, ANY TOWN AB1 2YZ

21-11-11

£ _____

SAMPLE

It says *seven million* so put 7 in the million slot.

million	hundred thousand	ten thousand	thousand	hundred	ten	unit
7						

It says *four thousand* so put 4 in the thousand slot.

million	hundred thousand	ten thousand	thousand	hundred	ten	unit
7			4			

It says *ten* so put 1 in the ten slot.

million	hundred thousand	ten thousand	thousand	hundred	ten	unit
7			4		1	

Now fill in the other slots with zeros, since the word number did not contain any other figures.

million	hundred thousand	ten thousand	thousand	hundred	ten	unit
7	0	0	4	0	1	0

The word number translates to a seven digit number 7 004 010
   Try a smaller number, thirty thousand and twenty four
   Read the number and start to fill in a place value grid.

Thirty thousand … put 3 in the ten thousands slot:

million	hundred thousand	ten thousand	thousand	hundred	ten	unit
		3				

and *twenty* … put 2 in the tens slot:

million	hundred thousand	ten thousand	thousand	hundred	ten	unit
		3			2	

four … put 4 in the units slot:

million	hundred thousand	ten thousand	thousand	hundred	ten	unit
		3			2	4

fill in the zeros:

million	hundred thousand	ten thousand	thousand	hundred	ten	unit
		3	0	0	2	4

The word number thirty thousand and twenty four writes out in symbols as 30 024

A way of checking your answer

There is a basic check you can make on whether or not you have written a number correctly. You count the number of digits (or sometimes the word 'figures' is used) in the number.

Sometimes you read in newspapers of people receiving a five figure or six figure salary. The number of figures/digits in a number gives some idea of the value of the number. So, the first (and lowest) five figure number is 10 000 and the last (and biggest) is:

99 999 … quite a big range!

The first six figure number is 100 000 and the last is 999 999 (one short of a million).

So, here is the check list:

- Hundreds are 3 figure/digit numbers
- Thousands are 4 figure/digit numbers
- Ten thousands are 5 figure/digit numbers
- Hundred thousands are 6 figure/digit numbers
- Millions are 7 figure/digit numbers
- Billions are 10 figure/digit numbers (A *billion* is a thousand millions)
- Trillions are 13 figure/digit numbers (A *trillion* is a thousand billions)

3   Counting and Number Sense

One of the first maths skills we should master is counting. If we learn it properly then it will help us to develop a sense of number, which is the first step to understanding maths.

The basic process of counting, as in chanting, 'One, two, three, four, five ...' does not teach us number sense. It merely teaches us the number words in the correct sequence. It is not dissimilar to learning the alphabet. That teaches us the letter names in sequence. It doesn't make us good readers or good spellers, unless we add in a lot more skills and knowledge. However, both these basic sequences are important to the development of understanding language or maths (but not necessarily essential for everyone).

What makes learning the number words different to learning the alphabet is that each word represents something, a quantity. What makes it similar is that combining two or more of these number words will help us to represent all the number quantities we will ever need in the same way that combining two or more letters will help us to represent all the words we will ever need.

Counting is a satisfactory procedure when we are dealing with small quantities, but it needs to be extended and developed as we approach bigger numbers.

If we continue to use counting one by one for big numbers it will be slow and probably inaccurate, so how can we build on this basic skill?

All maths facts and processes should be learned both forwards and backwards, for example, people should learn how to count backwards as well as forwards and learn, for example, that subtraction is like doing

addition backwards and that division is like doing multiplication, but backwards.

However, you may find that counting backwards is very much more of a challenge than counting forwards. If this so, then do not let it become a barrier to progress or a disincentive. Instead just practise counting back one step:

for example, for counting in ones, try ... 6, 7, 8, 9, 10 then 9 then 10, 11, 12 ...

for counting in twos, try ... 16, 18, 20 then 18 then 20, 22, 24 ...

or ... 7, 9, 11 then 9 then 11, 13, 15 ...

The main reason for asking you to practise counting backwards is to demonstrate how the operations of + − × and ÷ interlink with each other which in turn will help you to do maths.

How to develop counting skills

Counting in ones is an early skill. There are developments from this that will make your maths much more efficient and effective and probably a lot more accurate. These developments should also teach you more about what maths does and how to do it.

Start by counting and practising with ones. Forwards and then backwards if you can. If you want to use a visual aid count out 1p coins or maybe poker chips as these are easy to handle. Organise them in consistent patterns and when you get to 10 (p), exchange ten 1p coins for one 10p coin (or a different colour of poker chip). Continue the counting with more 1p coins.

Then move to counting in twos, the even number sequence, forwards and backwards (or just one step back and then forwards again)

$$2\ 4\ 6\ 8\ 10\ 12\ 14\ 16\ 18\ 20$$
$$20\ 18\ 16\ 14\ 12\ 10\ 8\ 6\ 4\ 2\ 0$$

Try adding a visual aid by counting out 2p coins. Set out the coins in the same patterns again.

When you get to 10 (10p) exchange the five 2p coins for a 10p coin. Continue counting with more 2p coins and look for the repeating pattern.

Counting in twos, the odd number sequence, forwards and backwards.

$$1\ 3\ 5\ 7\ 9\ 1\ 13\ 15\ 17\ 19$$
$$19\ 17\ 15\ 13\ 11\ 9\ 7\ 5\ 3\ 1$$

Again, try adding a visual and kinaesthetic aid by starting with a 1p coin, then count out 2p coins. When you get to 11 (p) exchange the five 2p coins for a 10p coin. Continue counting with more 2p coins and look for the repeating pattern in the numbers and the coins.

Practise these skills with coins or poker chips, by writing, by talking out loud, by talking under your breath. Practise when you are out walking or sitting in a room, by counting on objects in the room. Do not forget to try and count backwards as well as forwards. Build up pictures in your mind of what 5 objects, 7 objects, 10 objects etc look like. Ask yourself questions like, 'What is 2 more than 8?' or 'What is the number before 19?'

Now progress to counting in fives, again forwards and backwards.

$$5\ 10\ 15\ 20\ 25\ 30\ 35\ 40\dots$$
$$40\ 35\ 30\ 25\ 20\ 15\ 10\ 5\ 0$$

or mix directions

$$5\ 10\ 15\ 20\ 15\ 20\ 25\ 30\ 35\ 30\ 35$$

and look at the pattern in the coins and in the numbers. Could you do some exchanges of fives for tens? Two groups of 5 make 10, or a 10 could be split into two groups of 5.

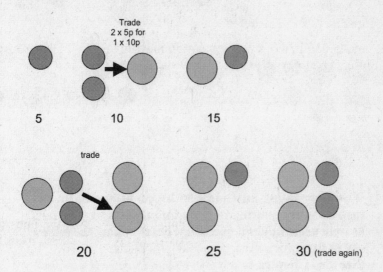

Finally practise how to count in tens.
   The basic sequence is

                10 20 30 40 50 60 70 80 90 100 …

But some people find it quite difficult to adapt this to a ten sequence that starts with a number other than 10, for example 13

                13 23 33 43 53 63 73 83 93 103 …

If you find this sequence difficult, simply keep the 3 in your memory and do the regular counting in tens, the add back the 3 when you have finished,

                14 … 10 20 30 40 50 60 70 80 90 100 … 103

From a place value perspective, you are adding to the tens column, but not to the units column so, naturally, the digit in the units column does not change. If you did this with 10p and 1p coins, it would look like this

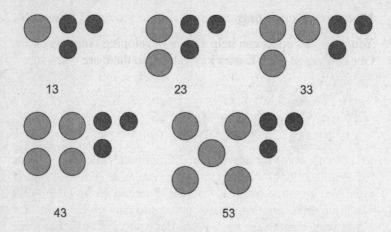

13   23   33

43   53

If you are doing any addition by counting on, do not restrict your counting to ones. Count on in fives or tens as well, using tallies if necessary, but grouping the tallies, say in fives.
(See also Chapter 4)
|||| ||||

The 'strike through' stroke makes the cluster of 4 |||| up to a cluster of 5 ||||.

I have deliberately not talked about counting in threes, fours, sixes, sevens, eights or nines. If you can master counting in these groups then that is just fine, but they are not essential skills, especially since it is possible to achieve the same outcome using counting in ones, twos, fives and tens. For example, counting in fours can be achieved via counting in twos and counting in nines can be achieved by counting on ten and then counting back one.

The goal is to keep all learning in your comfort zone and still be effective at maths.

Money and counting

You may find coins can help you in developing counting skills. Our coinage in the UK uses key values, so there are coins for:

1p 2p 5p
10p 20p 50p
£1 (100p) £2 (200p) £5 (500p)
£10 (1000p) £20 (2000p) £50 (5000p)

You can use coins for counting in different intervals and use them for trading to help you understand place value. For example, if you were counting in fives, you could trade two 5p coins for a 10p coin, or, if counting in twos you could trade five 2p coins for a 10p coin. Each trade to a 10p takes you up from units place value to tens place value.

You should practise the basic relationships illustrated by coins, that is:

4   is twice 2 or 2×2
5   is half of 10 or $10 \div 2$ or $4 + 1$
6   is $5 + 1$
7   is $5 + 2$
8   is $2 \times 2 \times 2$
9   is 1 less than 10
10 is 2×5

4 The Basic Building Blocks of Maths: the Basic + − × and ÷ Facts

Facts such as $7 + 8$ and $16 - 7$ are known as basic facts because they are the basis for all additions and subtractions. So if you know, for example, that $3 + 8 = 11$, then you will see this used again and again in any example involving 8 added to 3, such as

$3 + 8 = 11$
$13 + 8 = 21$ $3 + 18 = 21 \ (10 + 11)$
$23 + 18 = 41$ $13 + 28 = 41 \ (30 + 11)$
$30 + 80 = 110$ $300 + 800 = 1100$

This extended use of basic facts is very useful. What it means, in effect, is that you can take your knowledge of one fact into many other examples.

Many people are made to feel inadequate or even failures at maths from a very early age. This impression is then reinforced as their education progresses. One of the first reasons for this feeling of inadequacy is that they are asked to learn facts that they find hard to commit to memory.

It is a fact that not everyone can rote learn all the basic number facts,

especially if they have to recall them quickly. There is, as yet, no explanation as to why this is so.

It is better if you can get access to these basic number facts quickly, either by direct memory or by efficient strategies. You have to decide what works best for you. The time you spend on this task must be rewarding in terms of success or you will simply lose interest in the work.

For any topic in this book, never be afraid to move on for a while and then return back for another try. Sometimes knowing about the work ahead helps you to understand the earlier work.

Although rote learning is not a successful strategy for many people, it can be made effective for more people by using a technique devised and developed by a friend of mine, Dr Colin Lane. Let me describe this very powerful method for rote learning. As ever, it will not work for everyone, but then, nothing does.

The strategy is based on something many of us do when we are trying to remember a phone number if we do not have a pen and paper to write it down. You will probably keep repeating the number, under your breath. This is sub-vocalising and is the base of a learning technique called self-voice echo. Most of us learn best from hearing information in our own voice, hence self voice-echo. Some years ago I tested this out on some teenage males who knew very few times table facts, comparing self-voice echo with some other rote learning techniques. The self-voice group made the best gains, but even in that group there was one boy who did not make any gain. So, the best way to find out if self-voice echo will work for you is to give it a try. One way to do this is to use my CD-Rom, 'What to do when you can't learn the times tables' (see Appendix 3) which includes a section on self-voice echo.

If you can record the facts onto a PC and play them back as you see the facts on screen, then this too will give the multisensory experience that can sometimes make rote learning successful. Practise about five facts at each session. Make a session fairly short as this is a method that is quite demanding on your perseverance levels.

If even this powerful method of rote learning is not effective for you, there are other ways of accessing the more difficult facts by making efficient use of the facts that are easier to remember and the facts that are the most useful. Luckily these are often the same facts!

For example, look at two ways to approach the question, 'What is 5 + 6?'

First way: 'What is 5 + 6?'

Second way: 'What is 5 + 5? OK. It's 10. So what is 5 + 6?'

Did the second way make the question easier? If it did then you can improve your ability to access facts by making full use of a few key facts and inter-linking them to other 'harder' facts.

If you look at a table of the basic addition facts, there are 121 addition facts.

You do not need to learn all of these addition facts. It is possible to learn a few key facts and then use them to work out the others. Start in your comfort zone and work from there.

It is quick and efficient to count on for some of these facts. I think counting on 1,2 3 and even 4 is quick and acceptable as efficient for many adding tasks.

If you include adding on 0 as well, then this reduces what you need to learn from 121 facts to 36 facts.

	0	1	2	3	4	5	6	7	8	9	10
0	0	1	2	3	4	5	6	7	8	9	10
1	1	2	3	4	5	6	7	8	9	10	11
2	2	3	4	5	6	7	8	9	10	11	12
3	3	4	5	6	7	8	9	10	11	12	13
4	4	5	6	7	8	9	10	11	12	13	14
5	5	6	7	8	9	10	11	12	13	14	15
6	6	7	8	9	10	11	12	13	14	15	16
7	7	8	9	10	11	12	13	14	15	16	17
8	8	9	10	11	12	13	14	15	16	17	18
9	9	10	11	12	13	14	15	16	17	18	19
10	10	11	12	13	14	15	16	17	18	19	20

Of course this gain includes using, for example, 8 + 4 to work out 4 + 8 or using 7 + 2 to work out 2 + 7 as these pairs have the same result!

This 'two for the price of one' deal, which applies for addition facts almost halves the 36 facts left to go.

By inter-linking the easy facts to harder facts you can reduce this task even further, for example, the '+10' facts are easy because they follow a simple pattern, so as an example of the linking strategy mentioned before, let's link the +10 facts to the +9 facts.

The +10 facts follow a pattern and,

since 9 is (always) 1 less than 10, the +9 facts must follow a pattern,

but the answers for the +9 facts are (always) 1 less than the +10 facts.

Compare the answers in these two tables:

10 + 1 = 11	9 + 1 = 10	10 is 1 less than 11
10 + 2 = 12	9 + 2 = 11	
10 + 3 = 13	9 + 3 = 12	
10 + 4 = 14	9 + 4 = 13	
10 + 5 = 15	9 + 5 = 14	14 is 1 less than 15
10 + 6 = 16	9 + 6 = 15	
10 + 7 = 17	9 + 7 = 16	
10 + 8 = 18	9 + 8 = 17	17 is 1 less than 18
10 + 9 = 19	9 + 9 = 18	

So, to work out a +9 fact, take the linked +10 fact and take 1 off the +10 answer, for example:

For 9 + 7 start with 10 + 7 = 17 and subtract 1, answer is 16, so 9 + 7 = 16

If we fill in the +9 facts on the addition square that leaves just 10 facts to go!

Really useful addition facts.

In this book I keep returning to the same principle:

Take the facts you do know and use them to work out the facts you do not know.

Interestingly, that principle is just what all arithmetic is about even if you are a star performer. Very few people can remember every fact in arithmetic, for example, I doubt that many mathematicians have recall for the answer to 26 × 33 or indeed if that inability would in any way be a concern to them. What they can do is work it out using facts they do know.

So, why would we bother to remember everything when,
(a)   we can work it out, and
(b) we don't need that particular fact very often (if at all)
so, why waste memory space on it.

If you find learning number facts difficult then make sure that the facts you do learn are really useful.

For addition (and subtraction), the really useful facts are: the 'doubles' and the 'make ten'

THE DOUBLES:-

1 + 1 = 2   which are also a set of multiplication facts   2 × 1 = 2
2 + 2 = 4   2 × 2 = 4
3 + 3 = 6   2 × 3 = 6
4 + 4 = 8   2 × 4 = 8
5 + 5 = 10   ... *Look at this half way fact ... think of* **2 × 5 = 10**
6 + 6 = 12 5 *fingers on two hands as another 'visual'* 2 × 6 = 12
7 + 7 = 14   2 × 7 = 14
8 + 8 = 16   2 × 8 = 16
9 + 9 = 18   2 × 9 = 18
10 + 10 = 20   2 × 10 = 20

If we can organise information into patterns it makes the memory task easier (more efficient). The patterns may be oral (for example *six* times ten is *sixty*, *eight* times ten is *eighty*). The pattern may be visual (for example, it is easier to count the dots when in a visual pattern

You could use 2p coins to illustrate the pattern of counting in 2's, the doubles. Then, if you trade the $5 \times 2p$ coins for a 10p coin and count on another $5 \times 2p$ coins to get to 20, you see a repeat of the visual pattern. If you trade the $5 \times 2p$ coins again for a second 10p coin you can begin to see how the pattern for the units digits in the doubles continues forever.

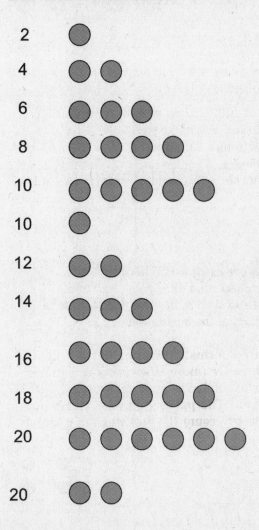

This pattern could also be done with the 2p coins organised as (see Chapter 3)

The 'make 10' facts
0 + 10 = 10
1 + 9 = 10
2 + 8 = 10
3 + 7 = 10
4 + 6 = 10
5 + 5 = 10 ... *look at this half way fact**... think of 5 fingers on 2 hands*
6 + 4 = 10
7 + 3 = 10
8 + 2 = 10
9 + 1 = 10
10 + 0 = 10

** Half way facts are extra useful because
(a) they can be a check that all is going well and,
(b) sometimes we can start at the half way point to save the time it takes to start at the beginning.

You could illustrate these 'make ten' facts with 1p coins.... Look at the visual pattern

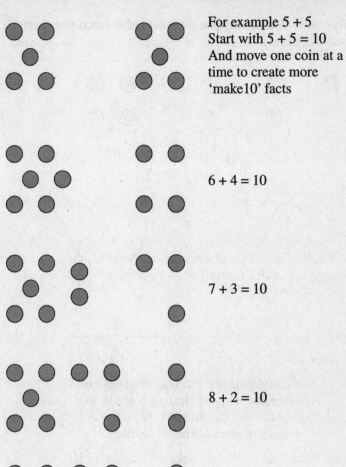

For example 5 + 5
Start with 5 + 5 = 10
And move one coin at a
time to create more
'make10' facts

6 + 4 = 10

7 + 3 = 10

8 + 2 = 10

9 + 1 = 10

You could use the fingers on your hands as an illustration of the 'make 10' facts (Figs 4.2 and 4.3) or you could imagine the number combinations written with sizes according to value (Fig 4.4)

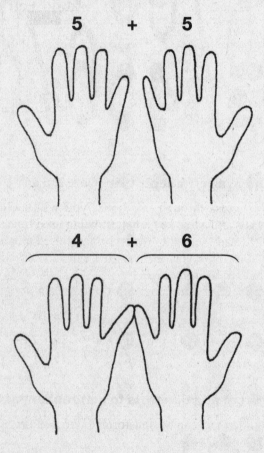

987654321
3456789
-12

The key numbers being used here are 2, 5 and 10.

As you progress through this book, you will see a few key number facts and a few key numbers being used time and again. You have already seen the 'Make 10' facts used to work out the 'Make 9' facts. Now you can learn to use the doubles for *'doubles plus 1'* and *'doubles minus 1'*

For example, if you know $6 + 6 = 12$, then you can access
$$6 + 7 = 12 + 1 = 13$$
and $6 + 5 = 12 - 1 = 11$
Or use $8 + 8 = 16$ to work out $8 + 9 = 16 + 1 = 17$
and $8 + 7 = 16 - 1 = 15$

Moving from addition facts to subtraction facts.

Every addition fact can be transformed into a subtraction fact.
For example: $7 + 3 = ?$
These symbols can be translated into words as:
'Seven plus three makes what?'
This same fact can be written as $7 + ? = 10$
This translates into words as:
'Seven plus what makes ten?'
which you can solve by adding on or counting on until you

reach 10. This counts on as 3 numbers, 8, 9, 10, so the answer is 3.

Counting on in this way is alternative way of subtracting and this 'make 10' fact now becomes:

$$10 - 7 = 3$$

$7 + 3 = ?$ can be transformed into $? + 3 = 10$

and using a similar argument as above, this changes to:

$$10 - 3 = 7$$

So if you know $7 + 3 = 10$ you can also create

$3 + 7 = 10$
$10 - 3 = 7$
$10 - 7 = 3$

You have used one fact to create 4 facts.

Addition facts can be seen and added in any order.

Addition facts can be rearranged to make subtraction facts.

Subtraction facts cannot be written in any order and still be correct.

For example,

$9 - 3 = 6$ but $3 - 9 = -6$ (*negative* or *minus* 6)

As we move through the basic facts for addition, subtraction, multiplication and division we shall use three guiding principles:

1. Using the key facts to work out other facts (and therefore frequently refreshing the key facts in your memory)
2. Breaking down and relating the operations ($+ - \times \div$)
3. Looking for patterns and relationships

Times table (or multiplication) facts

Recently I spoke with a very intelligent young woman who is studying maths at A level. She has been offered a place at Oxford University to study engineering. We were talking about her difficulties with some areas of maths and she recalled with great feeling and self awareness her experiences as a seven year old and being unable to commit the times tables to memory. All the children in her class who succeeded at this task received a special badge. She didn't and, although she can look back and see that this seems trivial now, at the time it had an enormous effect on her self-image of her ability to do maths. Sadly this story of low self-esteem for maths ability is not unique.

There are 121 times table facts, which can be presented as the traditional columns or tables, for example the four times table;

$1 \times 4 = 4$
$2 \times 4 = 8$
$3 \times 4 = 12$
$4 \times 4 = 16$
$5 \times 4 = 20$
$6 \times 4 = 24$
$7 \times 4 = 28$
$8 \times 4 = 32$
$9 \times 4 = 36$
$10 \times 4 = 40$

The times table facts can also be shown, altogether, in a table square.

	0	1	2	3	4	5	6	7	8	9	10
0	0	0	0	0	0	0	0	0	0	0	0
1	0	1	2	3	4	5	6	7	8	9	10
2	0	2	4	6	8	10	12	14	16	18	20
3	0	3	6	9	12	15	18	21	24	27	30
4	0	4	8	12	16	20	24	28	32	36	40
5	0	5	10	15	20	25	30	35	40	45	50
6	0	6	12	18	24	30	36	42	48	54	60
7	0	7	14	21	28	35	42	49	56	63	70
8	0	8	16	24	32	40	48	56	64	72	80
9	0	9	18	27	36	45	54	63	72	81	90
10	0	10	20	30	40	50	60	70	80	90	100

It is my experience that very few people know absolutely none of these facts. There is usually something to start work on! Whatever your own feelings about your level of achievement or otherwise in mathematics you will have learned at least some of these facts, usually the tables with the best patterns, that is the 0x, 1x, 2x, 5x and 10x. Surprisingly, if you use the table square as the way to present the facts rather than the separate times tables, it clearly shows that knowing these facts leaves only 36 facts to learn. In the second paragraph down I will show you how to reduce the remaining 36 by almost half with very little effort.

Traditional attitudes to learning the times tables leave many people feeling that the task is unachievable and that they are helpless to change that. In fact, if you look at what you do know, as I am explaining here, the 'unachievable' is not a huge task and can usually be achieved by simple strategies.

The reason why these 121 facts reduce to 36 is that each of those easy tables contain some of the facts from the harder tables. For example, from the seven times table facts these are; 0×7, 1×7, 2×7, 5×7 and 10×7.

The number of remaining facts on the table square is reduced even further by a useful maths idea, that is, you get the same answer to a multiplication of two numbers irrespective of which multiplies which. For example, 6×8 and 8×6 both give 48 and 3×4 and 4×3 both give 12. (This idea will be used again when I explain how to add and subtract fractions).

To explain this, try setting out 3×4 in 1p coins

Describing what you have depends on whether you look at rows or columns first. You can see that there are 4 rows of 3 or 3 columns of 4. Either way, there are 12 coins.

This relationship means that in most cases/facts, you get two facts for the price of one.

Let's get another quick gain, this time with the toughest fact in the times tables ..... 7×8 (and the same fact in its 8×7 form) . This particular fact is one of only two to follow a special pattern, a pattern of four consecutive numbers

5 6 7 8

can be modified to read

$56 = 7 \times 8$

The other fact that has a consecutive number sequence is $3 \times 4 = 12$

1 2 3 4

can be modified to read

$12 = 3 \times 4$

The easy steps strategy

The remaining missing facts can be treated by the same idea we used for addition facts, that is to use what you know to make one hard step into two easy steps. That is, we shall inter-relate the numbers, particularly by finding the 'easy' numbers in the harder numbers.

Fig 4.8 One hard step or two easy steps?

I shall also introduce you to the link between multiplication and addition, since this is one basis of the two easy steps methods.

Multiplication is the repeated addition of the same number. A times table fact such as 3×8 is the repeated addition of three eights, $8 + 8 + 8 = 24$.

3×8 is
$$\begin{array}{r} 8 \\ 8 \\ +8 \end{array}$$

This addition can be done one step at a time, but it is also easy to group the numbers as shown, that is 2×8 and 1×8.

So 3×8 is 2×8 (=16) plus one more 8, that is 24.

Another example:

6×6 is $6 + 6 + 6 + 6 + 6 + 6$

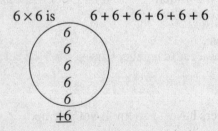

The 6's can be added one at a time or grouped into five 6's and one 6 as shown. This breaks down 6×6 into two easier steps

$5 \times 6 = 30$ and $1 \times 6 = 6$,
so $6 \times 6 = 36$
6 times 6 is 5×6 (=30) plus one more 6, that is 36.

This strategy is about looking for the easy numbers within the harder number. For times tables this is likely to be:

A 3× fact is calculated as a 2× fact plus a 1× fact (2 + 1 = 3).
A 6× fact is calculated as a 5× fact plus a 1× fact (5 + 1 = 6).
A 7× fact is calculated as a 5× fact plus a 2× fact (5 + 2 = 7).
A 4× fact is calculated as a 2× fact doubled (2 × 2 = 4).
A 5× fact can be calculated by dividing a 10× fact by 2 (10 ÷ 2 = 5).

This strategy also works with a subtraction. To take the 10× facts back to the 9× facts, a 9× fact is calculated as a 10× fact minus a 1× fact (10 − 1 = 9).

You take two facts you do remember and combine them to find facts you do not remember.

Using patterns in numbers

You can sometimes support your memory by finding patterns or relationships or links between facts, for example, the 9× table is a good table for patterns. The patterns take 9, a number that has an image of being difficult and make it a much friendlier number. As you may have guessed, patterns appeal to me. There are two reasons for this. One is they make the facts more secure in my mind. The second is that the pattern is teaching me something about understanding maths.

Let's look at the 9x table:

$1 \times 9 = 9$
$2 \times 9 = 18$
$3 \times 9 = 27$
$4 \times 9 = 36$ The answers have a pattern. If you add up

$5 \times 9 = 45$ the figures in any of the answers, the total is 9.
$6 \times 9 = 54$
$7 \times 9 = 63$ ... $6 + 3 = 9$
$8 \times 9 = 72$
$9 \times 9 = 81$ ... $8 + 1 = 9$
$10 \times 9 = 90$

There is another pattern in the answers to the nine times table. If you look down the unit figures in the answer column you can see how they sequence down as 9, 8, 7, 6, 5, 4, 3, 2, 1, 0. The figure in the tens column also sequence, but in the opposite direction, upwards, starting with an unwritten zero (in $1 \times 9 = 09$) and ending at 9.

The answer to any number times 9 will have digits which ultimately add up to make 9. For example, $85\ 461 \times 9 = 769\ 149$. Now add all the digits in the answer, $7 + 6 + 9 + 1 + 4 + 9 = 36$. Add again, $3 + 6 = 9$.

Now, let's try another pattern in the 9x table. This pattern works beyond just the table facts to multiplying any number by 9. Once again, we use the principle of taking a harder number and relate it to an easy number. We are going to use the 10x facts to take us to 9x facts.

This pattern is based on a relationship between 9 and 10. Nine is 1 less than 10, a relationship used on pages ** for extending basic addition facts and again on page ** for adding up shop prices.

You may find it helpful to use coins to illustrate the development of this idea. A 10p coin is 1p more than 9p. Change the order of this statement so that it reads that 9p is 1p less than 10p. If you took 2 ten pence coins, then 2 lots of 9p would be 2p less than these 2 ten pence coins. If you took 6 ten pence coins then 6 lots of 9p would be 6p less than the 6 ten pence coins.

I can show the link between the ten times table facts and the nine times table facts by building up the 9x table in comparison with the 10x table.

1 nine is 1 less than 1 ten	$1 \times 9 = 1 \times 10$ subtract 1
2 nines are 2 less than 2 tens	$2 \times 9 = 2 \times 10$ subtract 2
3 nines are 3 less than 3 tens	$3 \times 9 = 3 \times 10$ subtract 3
4 nines are 4 less than 4 tens	$4 \times 9 = 4 \times 10$ subtract 4
5 nines are 5 less than 5 tens	$5 \times 9 = 5 \times 10$ subtract 5
6 nines are 6 less than 6 tens	$6 \times 9 = 6 \times 10$ subtract 6
7 nines are 7 less than 7 tens	$7 \times 9 = 7 \times 10$ subtract 7
8 nines are 8 less than 8 tens	$8 \times 9 = 8 \times 10$ subtract 8
9 nines are 9 less than 9 tens	$9 \times 9 = 9 \times 10$ subtract 9

The pattern is shown in this table. If you need to work out a 9x fact, start with a 10x fact. For example, 6×9 starts with 6×10 equals 60 and then subtracts 6 to make 54.

You can check the answer by adding the figures. If they add to 9 you are correct and $5 + 4$ does make 9.

It may help you if you say the pattern, for example, 'One nine is one less than one ten. Two nines are two less than two tens. Three nines are three less than three tens. Four nines are four less than four tens...'

This strategy works for any number times 9. For example, try 35×9 ...

35×10 is 350.

Now subtract 35 from 350 to obtain 315.

Check by adding the digits in 315, $3 + 1 + 5$ which makes 9.

This method for working out the nine times table facts is a classic example of using two easy steps to achieve one difficult step. Of course if multiplying by nine is not a difficult step for you, you won't need to do this!

Another two step strategy can be used for multiplying (and dividing) by 4. To multiply by 4, you multiply by two, twice, for example to answer 4×7:

multiply 7 by 2 to give 14, then multiply by 2 again to get 28, that is

$$7 \times 2 = 14 \text{ followed by } 14 \times 2 = 28$$

To divide 784 by 4, use two steps:

$$784 \div 2 = 394 \text{ followed by } 392 \div 2 = 196$$

You could extend this by one more step (x 2) and then you can multiply and divide by 8.

Examinations

If you have to take a maths exam and you are not confident on retrieving the facts quickly from memory, especially in their division format, you may want to consider constructing your own table square from a blank 12×12 grid. This could be done at the start of the exam. You may not need to fill in all of it straight away, but enough to get you started. You could then fill in other facts as they cropped up in the exam.

Step 1. Set up a 12×12 grid
Step 2. Put in 0 – 10 across and down

	0	1	2	3	4	5	6	7	8	9	10
0											
1											
2											
3											
4											
5											
6											
7											
8											
9											
10											

Step 3. Fill in the 0×, 1× and 10× facts

Step 4. Fill in the 2× facts

Step 5. Fill in the 3× facts by adding the 2× facts to the 1× facts [for example for 3 ×

8 as 16 (2 × 8) plus 8 (1 × 8)]

Step 6. Fill in the 4× facts by doubling (×2) the 2× facts

Step 7. Fill in the 5× facts by counting or by halving the 10× facts

Step 8. Fill in the 6× facts by adding the 5× and 1× facts

Step 9. Fill in the 7× facts by adding the 5× and 2× facts

Step 10. 8 × 8 is 8 doubled three times… 16 … 32 … 64

5 Doing Stuff with Numbers: Add, Subtract, Multiply and Divide.

Mathematicians call add (+), subtract (-), multiply (×) and divide (÷) the *four operations*. These are the four basic ways you manipulate (operate on) numbers. If you can understand how the four operations work and how they inter-relate then you will have travelled a long way on your journey to understand maths.

Adding

Most people picture addition sums as looking something like these:

$$5 + 6 \qquad 29 + 37 \qquad \begin{array}{r} 436 \\ +278 \\ \hline \end{array} \qquad 23 + 68 + 93 + 77 + 84 + 12$$

but adding starts much earlier with the basic skill of counting.
If you count out loud the simple sequence of numbers, 1, 2, 3, 4, 5 … each new number in the sequence is obtained by adding 1.
Counting the even numbers, 2, 4, 6, 8 … is adding 2 each time.
  Counting in tens, 10, 20, 30, 40, 50 … is adding 10 each time.

  Adding is putting together. For example, putting together 5 coins and 3 coins gives a total of 8 coins.

Addition sums such as:

$$
\begin{array}{r}
56 \\
+23 \\
\hline
79
\end{array}
$$

involve putting together two numbers (for example, 56 and 23 to make a total of 79).

Subtracting

Subtracting usually conjures up images of sums such as:

$$9 - 3 \qquad 46 - 31 \qquad \begin{array}{r} 787 \\ -463 \\ \hline \end{array}$$

Subtraction is taking away, or separating, and there-fore it is the opposite of adding.

This means that counting back 10, 9, 8, 7, 6 is subtracting one each time.

Counting back 8, 6, 4, 2 is subtracting two each time.

Counting back 70, 60, 50, 40, 30 is subtracting ten each time.

The taking away and separating aspect of subtraction is illustrated in the following examples.

'If you had 8 coins and you take 3 away you have 5 left.'

You have separated the 8 coins into 3 coins and 5 coins.

Subtraction sums like:

$$
\begin{array}{r}
98 \\
-46 \\
\hline
52
\end{array}
$$

involve separating the number 98 into two parts. The number 46 is one part. By taking away 46 from 98 you find the second part, 52. The two parts do not have to be the same. They do not have to be equal parts.

Sometimes it is easier to subtract by counting on from the

subtract number up to the starting number, often using 10s. In the example above, you would

> start with 46 and add or count on 4 to reach 50
> continue from 50 and count on 40 in tens to reach 90
> count on a further 8 to reach 98
> or start with 46 and add or count on 2 to reach 48
> continue by adding tens until you reach 98, which will be 5 tens.

This makes an added on total of 52.

This is an example of linking two operations. You are using adding on to achieve a subtraction.

Multiplication

As we saw in the basic facts chapter, multiplication is a quick way of adding the same number several times, also known as 'repeated addition'. So there is a very close link between the two operations, addition and multiplication.

> **Multiplication is a process of adding together the same number several times. It is also known as 'repeated addition.'**

For example 7×6 is seven sixes added together, $6 + 6 + 6 + 6 + 6 + 6 + 6$.

Although it would be possible, and mathematically correct to work out 7×6 by adding up 6 seven times, it is quicker and probably more accurate to know the answer is 42 or to work it out by a more efficient method than doing seven separate additions. For example, you could use two facts that are easier to remember and add them. In this case the two facts might be 5×6 and 2×6, so

$$7 \times 6 \text{ is broken down into } 5 \times 6 \text{ plus } 2 \times 6$$
$$(6 + 6 + 6 + 6 + 6) + (6 + 6)$$

It will make multiplication much easier to understand if you realise how it is so closely related to adding, that multiplication is really a special form of addition.

The method most people learned at school called 'long multi-plication' is really a mixture of addition and multiplication. I will explain this in more detail on page*.

Division

Division is about dividing a number into equal parts. It is the opposite of multiplication. This means it is also repeated sub-traction, taking away the same number several times.

For example, to divide 36 by 9, you could take away 9s suc-cessively until you reach zero:

$$36 - 9 = 27$$
$$27 - 9 = 18$$
$$18 - 9 = 9$$
$$9 - 9 = 0$$

Four 9's were taken away, so $36 \div 9 = 4$

If the division by repeatedly subtracting the same number gets to be too many steps, it may be possible to subtract 'easy' groups of the number, for example, to divide 153 by 9 you might take away 10×9

$153 - 90 = 63$ **10 lots of 9**

then 5×9
$63 - 45 = 18$ **5 lots of 9**

then 2×9
$18 - 18 = 0$ **2 lots of 9**

which means you have subtracted $10 + 5 + 2$ lots of 9, so $153 \div 9 = 17$

You might even get sophisticated enough to mix subtraction and addition for multiplying and dividing, for example

19×13 could be viewed as 20×13 subtract 1×13

This could also be phrased or said as '19 lots of 13 is also 20 lots of 13 subtract 1 lot of 13.'

$19 \times 13 = 20 \times 13 - 1 \times 13 = 260 - 13 = 247$

$117 \div 13$ could be calculated by starting with $13 \times 10 = 130$ which means $130 \div 13 = 10$. This also gives you a first estimate. Since 117 is less than 130, then the answer will be less than 10, but not a lot, in fact it is 13 less, so the answer must be 9.

I hope you can see how the four operations, add, subtract, multiply and divide are closely related and how they can be mixed and blended to suit the way you want to work.

One of the biggest misconceptions about mathematics is that there is only one way to do something. It is possible to use ideas such as the link between addition, subtraction, division and multiplication to provide alternate methods of calculation.

The traditional methods for addition and subtraction

These are the written methods that involve 'carrying' and 'borrowing' and 'decomposing'. These words are a good illustration of the point I made on page 9 about the language of maths. They all have other meanings that have nothing to do with maths. For example, you may well have developed your own understanding for the word 'borrowing' and that could handicap the way it is interpreted for maths use.

The first time we meet something new and learn it is a very powerful entry into our brains, so new interpretations may not be acceptable to our brain.

Never-the-less, I shall now embark on explanations which will use these words because they are likely to be the ones that were used to teach you. I shall also introduce an alternative, which I think does a better job.

I shall work through, in detail, the addition of two numbers to get a total and then do the same for a subtraction using the same numbers and taking the total apart again. This should illustrate again that addition and subtraction are the same processes in reverse. It might even make the 'carrying' and 'decomposing' clearer. I have used coins to help illustrate the procedures. You may want to use coins yourself as you work through the examples. You may find that the coins do the job, or you may be happy with just the symbols. Find the way that works for you!

So, even if you think you are an expert at addition, humour me, and work through the explanation.

Note how the coins are pictured in the familiar pattern I have constantly used for 5. Once again we are focusing on 2, 5 and 10.

The addition example is:

$$\begin{array}{r} 187 \\ +269 \\ \hline \end{array}$$

To help you develop a clear picture of the steps, try using 1p coins (for units), 10p coins (for tens) and £1 coins (for hundreds).

Set up the coins.

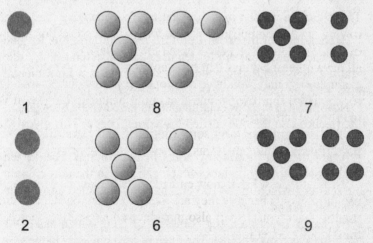

In the written method you start on the right with the units. Since addition is putting together, move the 7 one pence coins and 9 one pence coins together. This gives 16 coins.

Having 16 coins in the units column is a problem, because 16 is made up of six units, which is fine, but also one ten and that ten obviously belongs in the tens column. We deal with this by exchanging ten 1p coins for one 10p coin and, in old language, 'carry' the ten into the tens column.

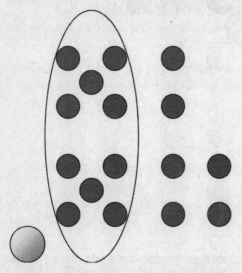

Exchanging, or the word I prefer, *'trading'* ten units for one ten, or backwards, one ten for ten units, and also ten tens for one hundred, one hundred for ten tens and so on is a fundamental process in numeracy.

Now move to the tens column and put together the 8 ten pence, 6 ten pence and the one carried/traded ten pence. This gives 15 ten pence coins.

Again there are too many coins in the column. The 15 ten pence coins represent 5 tens, which can stay in the tens column and ten tens which make 100 and have to be traded up into the hundreds column.

Exchange (trade) ten 10p coins for £1 coin, which makes £1 and 50p (5 ten pence coins). The 5 ten pence coins stay in the tens column and the pound (hundred) is moved (carried) to the hundreds column.

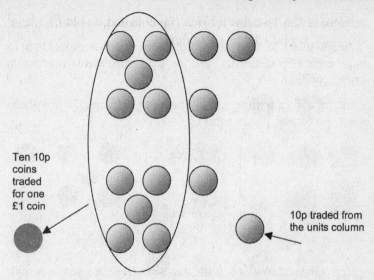

Ten 10p
coins
traded
for one
£1 coin

10p traded from
the units column

All that remains is to put together the hundreds, the £1 coins.
Add together the 1 and the 2 from the sum and add in the carried
1 to make 4 hundreds. The addition is complete.

$$
\begin{array}{r}
187 \\
+269 \\
\hline
456
\end{array}
$$

It should help your understanding of the processes of addition
if you use the coins to demonstrate each step. The coins follow
exactly the same process as the written method and this makes
them a useful link to the symbols/numbers.

I want to show you that subtraction is the reverse of addition
and so this subtraction example below uses the same numbers as
I used for addition, but now we shall separate the total into its two
parts again.

    456   which was the total
  -187   which was one of the parts
   ???   which is the answer and will be the other part

What the question actually 'says' is;

'Here is 456, take away 187 and find out what is left.'

Again, using coins to work through the question should help to make each step clear, because the coin movements mirror the written method.

Set up 456 in writing and in coins (4× £1 coins, 5× ten pence coins and 6× one pence coins).

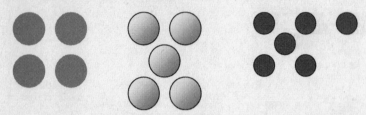

The subtraction starts with the units (the one pence coins). You have to take away 7 coins from the 6. Obviously 6 is smaller than 7, making this subtraction a little tricky (well, impossible!) without some adjustment to the coins.

You need to obtain some more 1p coins, so you reverse the trading you did for the addition. Exchange or trade a ten pence coin for ten 1p coins. This takes the number of ten pence coins down from 5 to 4 and puts 10 extra one pence coins into the units place so that now there are 16 one pence coins in the units place. School textbooks call this 'decomposition' because you have decomposed the 456 into four hundreds, four tens and sixteen units. I prefer 'trading' because it is a word that applies to both the addition and the subtraction procedures.

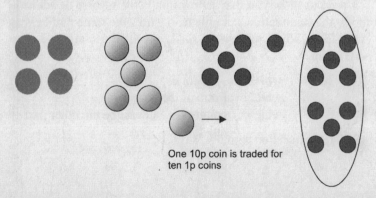

One 10p coin is traded for
ten 1p coins

Now you can take away 7 one pence coins, leaving 9 one pence coins. 9 is the units digit of your answer.

Move on to the tens ...

There are now 4 tens and you need to take away 8. As 4 is less than 8, again you have to trade (decompose the number). So do the opposite trade you did for the addition. Trade one of the £1 (hundred) coins for ten 10p coins. This leaves 3 hundreds (three £1 coins) in the hundreds column. Put the ten 10p coins in the tens column to make 14 ten pence coins altogether.

Now you can take away 8 tens, leaving 6 as the tens digit of your answer.

The last step is to subtract in the hundreds column. There are 3 hundreds (three £1 coins) left. Take away 1 to leave 2 hundreds as your answer in the hundreds place value column.

$$\begin{array}{r} 456 \\ -187 \\ \hline 269 \end{array}$$

The final answer is 269, which, of course is the number you added to 187 to make 456.

This decomposition or trading method breaks down a number into parts that are more suitable for the subtraction. Breaking down numbers is a technique that is often useful in maths. This particular breaking down technique is aimed to produce enough units, or tens, or hundreds, etc to make a subtraction possible.

In 456 the units and the tens figures were not large enough for the subtraction. So we decomposed or renamed the 456 as

3 hundreds, 14 tens and 16 units

This is still 456 ...
$$\begin{array}{rl} 300 & \text{3 hundreds} \\ 140 & \text{14 tens} \\ +16 & \text{16 units} \\ \hline 456 & \end{array}$$

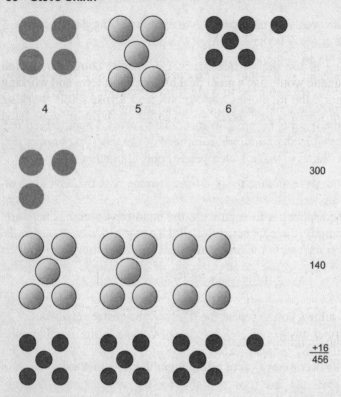

4   5   6

300

140

+16
456

So, this is another example of maths using the 'breaking down and building up numbers' strategy in order to make a calculation easier.

Here are two ways to write down this method of subtraction;

3^14
the messy 4 5^{1}6   or adding in a middle line   4 5 6
          −1 8 7   3 14 16
           2 6 9   −1 8 7
                                                       2 6 9

Other ways of doing subtraction including mental maths.

Trying to use the written method described above for mental arithmetic would ask a great deal of your short term and working memory, the memories you would need to use while working out this subtraction, holding the different digits in your head while you move through each step.

There is another disadvantage in using the method described above for mental arithmetic. In this written method you work from units to hundreds, so you move from right to the left as you do each step. This means you have to hold the unit and tens digits in your brain, with no practise or repetition as you move on to new digits. That may well overload your memory as it tries to hold on the earlier digits whilst working on the new digits. Then the final answer requires you to present these digits in the reverse order to the way you used them in the calculation.

So, you could work in the direction from hundreds to units. This allows you to repeat the digits as the answer evolves.

The 'hundreds to units' method:

The explanation takes a lot longer than the method!

456 – 187.
Start at the hundreds:
4 (hundred) minus 1 (hundred) = 3 (hundred)

Move to tens:
35 (tens or three hundred and fifty) minus 8 (tens) … you could do this by taking 10 tens and adding back 2 tens to give 27 tens or
the answer, so far is two hundred and seventy

Move to units:
276 (units) minus 7 (units) … you could take 10 units (1 ten) from the two hundred and seventy six, leaving two hundred and sixty six then add back 3

Alternatively you could just take 7 from 276

The answer is 269

The adding on method.

Now try the adding on method, which again uses the fact that addition and subtraction are reversals of the same idea. It also uses number bonds for 10.

Using 456 – 187 again:
Start at 187 and add on numbers until you reach the target number of 456. Use sensible stages: go for tens and hundreds.

187 plus 3 is 190
190 plus 10 is 200 … so far 13 added on
200 plus 200 is 400 … so far 213 added on
400 plus 56 is 456 … 213 + 56 is 269 added on.

You could add the 56 in two stages, first 50, then 6.

This method uses a running total. The repetition of the numbers at each stage helps the short term memory to retain the numbers.

This is also a good method for working out change, for example, the change from £10 if you buy an item costing £4.49:

Start at £4.49

Add on 1p   £4.50
Add on 50p   £5.00
Add on £5   £10.00

The total added on is 1p + 50p + £5, £5.51

Two ways to add a column of numbers

This is a difficult task for many people. If they use a calculator, they often make a mistake at one stage and get the total wrong. The two methods described below are quite different from each other, but both provide real support for the adding process.

1. The tally method
   Once more, the description of 'how to do it' is longer than the

method. This particular method tends to appeal to inchworms rather than grasshoppers. It uses tallies (as slashes) to reduce the load on memory.

$$
\begin{array}{r}
4 \\
46 \\
7\!\!\!/8 \\
65 \\
9\!\!\!/3 \\
28 \\
57 \\
5\!\!\!/6 \\
+36 \\
\hline
459
\end{array}
$$

Start at the top of the units column and add 6 + 8 = 14. Draw a slash through the 8 (this tally represents the ten from 14) and carry on adding down with the 4 (from the 14) added to the 5 to make 9. Next number 3 + 9 = 12. Draw a slash through the 3 (this tally represents the ten from the 12) and carry on adding down, 2 + 8 = 10. Draw a slash through the 8 to represent another ten. Add on down 7 + 6 = 13. Another slash, through the 6. Add on down 3 + 6 = 9. The 9 goes in the units column as its total.

Now count the tally marks (slashes). There are four, 4, tallies. This represents 4 tens to write at the top of the tens column.

Now add down the tens column using the same tally method, but each tally mark is now worth one hundred, 100.

4 + 4 = 8. Then 8 + 7 = 15, so a slash through the 7 represents a hundred and the 5 is carried on. 5 + 6 = 11. A slash through the 6 represents another 100.

Carry on adding down the column. 1 + 9 = 10. Another slash for another 100, through the 9. Adding down again, 2 + 5 = 7. Then 7 + 5 = 12. Draw a slash for another 100 through the 4.

2 + 3 = 5. Write 5 as the total of the tens column.

Count the slashes / tallies for the 100's. There are four, 4.

Write 4 as the total in the hundreds column.

This makes the final answer 459.

2. *The casting out tens method*

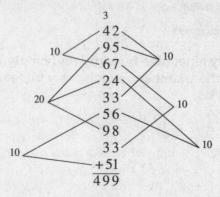

In this method you look within each column for pairs or triples of numbers that add up to 10 or 20. It is a method that uses the number combinations for 10 again.

Look for the number combinations for 10 in the units column:

$2 + 5 + 3 = 10$ ... cross out 2, 5 and 3
$7 + 3 = 10$ ... cross out 7 and 3
$4 + 6 = 10$ ... cross out 4 and 6

so there are 3 number combinations for 10
The only numbers left are $8 + 1 = 9$.
So 9 is written as the total for the units column.

The 3 from the 3 tens is written at the top of the tens column. Look for the number combinations for 10 in the tens column:

$4 + 6 = 10$ ... cross out 4 and 6
$9 + 2 + 9 = 20$ ... cross out 9, 2 and 9
$5 + 5 = 10$ ... cross out 5 and 5

so there are 4 number combinations for ten in the tens column (which is really 4 lots of 100 or 400)

All that is left to add in the tens column is $3 + 3 + 3 = 9$.

So 9 is the total for the tens column (90).

The 4 (tens combinations making 4 hundreds) is written in the hundreds column.

The answer is 499.

Nine, ninety nine, nine hundred and ninety nine and all those other numbers which are a bit less than 10, 100 and 1000.

Inchworms do not like 9, 99 and 999 and similar numbers in this range, such as 95 or 997. If they are or have been inchworms who rely on finger counting, then any numbers involving 9 will remind them of counting a lot of fingers.

Grasshoppers quite like these numbers, because the grasshopper sees relationships in numbers. A grasshopper relates numbers to each other, seeking number relationships and combinations that lead to easier numbers (for a grasshopper). So grasshoppers perceive 9 is close to 10. 99, 98, 97, 96 and 95 are close to 100. 999, 998, and 997 and so on are pictured as close to 1000.

The grasshopper will have a better time with mental arithmetic especially when it involves these type of numbers. Inchworm educationalists who set examinations (and you can tell they are inchworms by the questions they create) will rub their hands in sadistic glee as they pile on the 9's in the questions they see as difficult for other inchworms. There is no loyalty or empathy among some inchworms, or maybe it is just an exam setter's thing.

For mental arithmetic questions involving these numbers, it is worth everyone learning some grasshopper techniques. Inchworms will by their nature try to use their written methods to do mental arithmetic and many of these methods will make too much demand on their (short term and working) memories for them to succeed. It is hard for an inchworm to adopt grasshopper methods (and vice-versa), but it is worth them persevering and overcoming the feeling that if it is easier they must be cheating.

To illustrate this let's return to an example similar to that on page 61. I will explain how an inchworm and a grasshopper solve a mental subtraction, 522 – 98. As I explain each method, think about the demands of the method on short and long term memory.

The inchworm would rather do this sum (or any sum) on paper. Since this is not allowed in mental maths, the inchworm will try to replicate the written method in his head. He starts by visualising the question as he would write it

$$\begin{array}{r} 522 \\ -98 \\ \hline \end{array}$$

The next step depends on whether he uses renaming (decomposition) or the equal additions method. Let's say he uses renaming:

$$\begin{array}{r} ^4\ ^{11} \\ \cancel{5}\,\cancel{2}\,{}^{1}2 \\ -9\ \ 8 \\ \hline \end{array}$$

Now, holding all this in his memory, he subtracts to obtain 424.

The grasshopper sees the 98 as 2 less tham100, subtracts 100 to get 422 and adds back 2, since subtracting 100 gave a smaller answer than subtracting 98. Answer 424.

Grasshoppers make great use of the 'Is the answer going to be bigger or smaller?' question, both during the calculation and for checking their final answer.

The same principles can be used when shopping. For example, books tend to be priced as £6.99, £14.99, or some amount pounds and 99p. Inchworms will simply try to add the prices as written, which is quite difficult in that such an addition has many steps. Grasshoppers will round up each price, for example, £6.99 to £7 and £14.99 to £15, add them to get £22 and then, if they consider the detail worth it, readjust to an accurate answer (£21.98).

Again, a grasshopper will add:
£4.95 + £19.95 + £6.95 as £5 + £20 + £7 to a total of £32.
The readjustment is by subtracting $3 \times 5p = 15p$ from £32 to give £31.85.

This example shows how the numbers have been simplified to

give a reduced number of figures so that, if trying to work this out mentally, the load on memory is greatly reduced.

Another grasshopper skill is the clustering or pairing of less easy numbers into easy numbers, for example ten (see page ** for another use of this strategy).

The following example appears in a GCSE maths textbook. 'Add together mentally, 9, 2, 3 and 6.' The book then goes on to add them one at a time in the order given.

If you look at these numbers, that is you take time to overview them, the 3 and 6 make 9, the 2 can be split into 1 and 1, making the two 9's into two tens and the answer into 20.

$$
\begin{array}{cccc}
9 & 2 & \underline{3} & \underline{6} \\
9 & 2 & 9 & \\
\underline{9} & 1\ 1 & \underline{9} & \\
& \underline{10} & \underline{10} & \\
& 20 & &
\end{array}
$$

Multiplying by 10, 100, 1000, 10 000 and more

This is a useful and easy process. It is easy because it follows a simple pattern. First I will show you the pattern. Then I'll explain the maths behind the pattern. Look at these two *whole number* examples:

$43 \times 10 = 430$
$43 \times 100 = 4300$
$43 \times 1000 = 43\ 000$
$43 \times 10\ 000 = 430\ 000$
$43 \times 100\ 000 = 4\ 300\ 000$
$72 \times 10 = 720$
$72 \times 100 = 7200$
$72 \times 1000 = 72\ 000$
$72 \times 10\ 000 = 720\ 000$
$72 \times 100\ 000 = 7\ 200\ 000$

The pattern is in the zeros. The number of zeros on each side of the equals sign are the same.

The pattern is, like any good pattern, predictable. When you multiply by 100, with its two zeros, these two zeros appear in the answer, pushing place values up by 100 times, that is two place values. When you multiply by 1000, with its three zeros, these three zeros appear in the answer, pushing place values up by 1000 times.

The maths is simple (trust me).

If a number is multiplied by 10 it gets 10 times bigger. If a number is multiplied by 100 it gets 100 times bigger.. If a number is multiplied by 1000 it gets 1000 times bigger. And so on.

How do we know a number is 10 times bigger, or 100 times bigger, or 1000 times bigger, or so on?

There are two points to look for. The first is that the digits in the number are the same, but have some zeros tacked on the end. The second (which is more generally applicable) is that the place values of the digits in the number have increased. For example, if you select the 4 from the 43. In 43, the 4 represents 40. The 4 has a tens place value.

In $43 \times 10 = 430$, the 4 moves from a tens place value to a hundreds place value.

In $43 \times 100 = 4300$, the 4 has moved from a tens place value to a thousands place value.

In $43 \times 1000 = 43\ 000$, the 4 has moved from a tens place value to a ten thousands place value.

After the section on decimal numbers we can look at multiplying decimal numbers and dividing whole numbers or decimal numbers by 10, 100, 1000, 10 000 and so on.

Long multiplication, or a confusing mixture of addition and multiplication

Somewhere, sometime, someone probably explained long multiplication to you. You were probably too young at the time to appreciate the structure of the procedure. I always felt it had a 12 certificate, but was forced onto a PG audience.

Short multiplication is one step, for example $10 \times 5 = 50$ is definitely one step. $16 \times 2 = 32$ is one step for most, but ...

Long multiplication is definitely more than one step, but it is just another version of the strategy I described for working out 6 × 4 (page 41). For 6 × 4, the multiplication was related to repeated addition, addition of 4 six times.

$$
\begin{array}{r}
4 \\
4 \\
4 \\
4 \\
4 \\
+\,4 \\
\hline
\end{array}
$$

To avoid a step by step addition of 4 + 4 + 4 + 4 + 4 + 4, the sum can be grouped as 5 × 4 plus 1 × 4, which is a mixture of addition and multiplication.

This technique can be extended to other multiplications, for example,

12 × 7, which is 7 + 7 + 7 + 7 + 7 + 7 + 7 + 7 + 7 + 7 + 7 + 7

The twelve 7's can be clustered into two groups, one of ten 7's and one of two 7's

$$12 \times 7 \quad \text{is} \quad 10 \times 7 \quad \text{plus} \quad 2 \times 7$$

The multiplication has been broken down into two easier parts, 10 × 7 (=70) and 2 × 7 (=14). The answers to the two parts are added (70 + 14) to give the total answer as 84.

This procedure extends into 'long multiplication'. I interpret 'long' as meaning more than one step in the procedure. In long multiplication, the multiplication process is broken down into manageable parts. The traditional break down is automatic in the sense it is prescribed by what we are taught and is an 'only one way' method. It tells us to split the numbers according to their place values.

For example, to multiply 58 by 46, we split the 46 into 40 and 6, so that the two steps for the procedure are that you multiply 58 by 40 and then you multiply 58 by 6. Then you add the two parts together.

Or to multiply 521 by 426, the split is to multiply 521 by 400, then you multiply 521 by 20 and then third multiplication, 521 by 6.

The answers to these three partial multiplications are then added to show the answer for the full multiplication 521 by 426.

For example: 48×35

We split the 35 into 30 and 5 and do two partial multiplications:

$48 \times 30 = 1440$
$48 \times 5\ \ = \ \ 240$

We add the two parts to get the full answer:

$1440 + 240 = 1680$

This is traditionally set out as shown below:

```
      48
    × 35
    1440    this is 48 × 30
     240    this is 48 ×  5
    1680    this is 48 × 35
```

I have found that a visual image can sometimes help with understanding this multiplication. A calculation like 48×35 is the same as a calculation to work out the area of a rectangle with sides of 48 and 35.

48

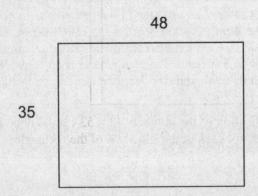

35

If the rectangle is broken down into two sub-areas, using the place value split into units and tens for 35, you have a picture of the two parts of the multiplication.

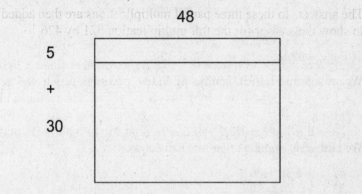

It is also possible to split a rectangle into four sub-areas and do the multiplication in four parts.

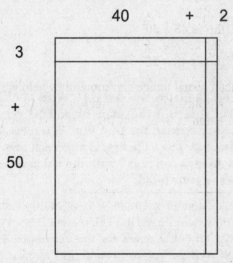

So, the multiplication of the numbers 42×53 can be done in four parts, one part for each of the sub areas of the rectangle.

42×53

a) $40 \times 50 = 2000$

b) $40 \times 3 = 120$ The four parts are added to make the

c) $2 \times 50 = 100$ full answer.

d) $\underline{2 \times 3 = 6}$

$42 \times 53 = 2226$

Using a rectangle to represent a two figure number times a two figure number multiplication provides a picture which can be used again as maths develops into new topics, for example in algebra.

As a third alternative, you can look at the two numbers and find the easy numbers that make them up.

42   2 + 20 + 20

53   1 + 2 + 50

Both splits give you three steps to the final answer, each step using easy multiplications.

$53 \times 2 = 106$

$53 \times 20 = 1060$

$\underline{53 \times 20 = 1060}$

$53 \times 42 = 2226$

So many times in maths, an idea is recycled in different disguises, but it is still the same idea. This recycling helps you to understand the first time you meet a new, extended idea, but it also illustrates how each new interpretation of an idea can make both the old and the new idea stronger in your mind.

Now, let us look a longer example of long multiplication. It is unlikely that you would do such a calculation in everyday life. You would most probably reach for the calculator. However, some exams may well ask you to do a multiplication of this complexity. The principles remain the same. There are just more steps on the way to the answer.

$$637 \times 736$$

Tradition requires us to break down the 736 into hundreds, tens and units

$$736 \text{ is } 700 + 30 + 6$$

and thus do three part multiplications, which are then added together:

$$637 \times 700 = 445900 \qquad 637 \times 30 = 19110 \qquad 637 \times 6 = 3822$$

$$445900 + 19110 + 3822 = 468832$$

This is traditionally set out as shown below:

$$
\begin{array}{r}
637 \\
\times\,736 \\
\hline
445900 \\
19110 \\
3822 \\
\hline
468832 \\
\end{array}
$$

    this is $637 \times \mathbf{700}$
    this is $637 \times \mathbf{\ \ 30}$
    this is $637 \times \mathbf{\ \ \ \ 6}$
    this is $637 \times \mathbf{736}$

There are occasions when you might combine multiplication with a subtraction, for example with a multiplication like 475×299. Rather than break down 299 into 200, 90 and 9, it is easier to break 299 into 300 and 1 and subtract $(300 - 1 = 299)$.

$$475 \times 300 = 142\,500 \qquad\qquad 475 \times 1 = 475$$

$$475 \times 299 = 142\,500 - 475 = 142\,025$$

This variation requires you to look at the dividing number in a non-formula way. If you have been drilled to do 'long' multiplication in steps of units, tens and hundreds, then you are likely to just leap in and multiply as 200x, 90x and 9x.

In order to make maths easier, you have to step back, control your urge to leap into using a formula straight away, and look at the numbers in the problem. Then ask yourself, 'Can I find easier ways for these numbers?'

The traditional method of long multiplication as shown above is fine if you know all your times table facts. If you do not then it is not a good method for you. Also you are much more likely to make mistakes in recalling those facts when you are in the middle of a complex problem, like long multiplication.

If you look for the easy numbers that make up the numbers in your problem, you can avoid having to use the difficult numbers!

In our example, 637×736, we should look at both numbers

637 has $500 + 100 + 20 + 10 + 5 + 2$
736 has $500 + 200 + 20 + 10 + 5 + 1$

Both numbers break down into six 'easy' numbers, so we can work out an answer using six easy multiplications, rather than three difficult multiplications. If that is a better alternative for you, then this is what you do:

736×1 =   736
736×2 =   1472
736×5 =   3680   (which you can do by 736×5 or by $7360 \div 2$)
736×10 =   7360
736×20 =   14720
736×100=   73600
736×500= 368000

500	368000
100	73600
20	14720
10	7360
5	3680
+2	+1472
637	468832

(Remember that when adding columns of numbers you can cast out number combinations for 10. This works well for this example.)

Indices

Indices are another bit of maths code. They are used when multiplying together same numbers. Look at these two examples:

the area of a square which has sides of length 5 is 5×5

5×5 is also written as 5^2 (see also page 141)

This is also named as 'five squared' or 'five to the power of 2'

Then we progress to the volume of a cube which has sides of length 5.

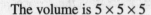

The volume is $5 \times 5 \times 5$

$5 \times 5 \times 5$ can be also written as 5^3

This is also called 'five cubed' or 'five to the power of 3'
  If you follow this pattern logically, you will write

  $5 \times 5 \times 5 \times 5$ as 5^4

This is also expressed as 'five to the power of four'
  So this pattern is predictable, for example, eight fives multiplied together would be written

$5 \times 5 \times 5 \times 5 \times 5 \times 5 \times 5 \times 5$ or 5^8

Indices are especially useful with powers of ten. This time I shall show that the logic of the sequential pattern can be taken forwards and backwards. First the forwards pattern:

$10 \times 10 = 10^2 = 100$
$10 \times 10 \times 10 = 10^3 = 1000$ a thousand is 10^3
$10 \times 10 \times 10 \times 10 = 10^4 = 10\ 000$

$10 \times 10 \times 10 \times 10 \times 10^5 = 10 = 100\ 000$
$10 \times 10 \times 10 \times 10 \times 10 \times 10 = 10^6 = 1\ 000\ 000$ a million is 10^6

Now the backwards pattern:

$1000 = 10 \times 10 \times 10 = 10^3$
$100 = 10 \times 10 = 10^2$
$10 = 10 = 10^1$
$1 = 10^0$
$0.1 = \frac{1}{10} = 10^{-1}$
$0.01 = \frac{1}{100} = \frac{1}{10 \times 10} = 10^{-2}$
$0.001 = \frac{1}{1000} = \frac{1}{10 \times 10 \times 10} = 10^{-3}$

The division by powers of 10 is shown by using a – (minus or negative) sign in front of the indices.

Division the easier way.

Wherever I lecture around the world, the procedure called 'long' division such as $24\overline{)12744}$ or $12744 \div 24$) is generally considered to be difficult. If long multiplication has a 12 certificate, long division, in its traditional format, has a 15, verging on 18 certificate. It certainly requires you to use a lot of maths sub skills.

Of course, you can use a calculator, but if you do you should always be able to do at least a rough mental check to give an estimate. Division on a calculator often results in using the keys in the wrong order. For example, with $24\overline{)12744}$ the correct order for keying into the calculator is (1) 12744 (2) ÷ (3) 24 and (4) = This is a change in the order in which the sum was presented.

There is an alternative method (which also happens to have a built-in estimate). I give this a PG, maybe 12 certificate.

The method is based on multiplication and division being the same procedure, but opposite. A basic example should explain this …

Seven times nine equals sixty three $7 \times 9 = 63$

This fact also tells us that there are seven nines in sixty three which is one of the ways of saying that sixty three divided by nine is seven.

$63 \div 9 = 7$

(It also tells us that sixty three divided by seven is nine. $63 \div 7 = 9$. Every multiplication fact is two division facts).

So if 63 is to be divided by 9, you could look at this sum as a multiplication with one number missing (the answer)

$63 = 9 \times ?$

This missing multiplier is the basis of the method for division.

for example, in the division $23\overline{)11776}$

23 is the dividing number, and the answer to the division is the other multiplying factor as in $23 \times ?? = 11776$

In other words, in this method you are finding out what number multiplies the dividing number to give the original number, so the example becomes

$11776 = 23 \times ??$

The division has been turned into a multiplication, another example of the usefulness of rewording maths questions. This is the first stage of this alternate method for division.

The next stage is to set up a simple table of easy multiples of 23. *Once again we shall focus on 1, 2, 5, 10, 20 and so on.* Look for the pattern in the numbers in the table. Can you see the relationship between 5×23 and 50×23 or between 5×23 and 10×23? Also the number of zeros in each multiple shows when you have multiplied 23 by 10, 100 or 1000 (see page 68). These patterns give you ways of checking that you are getting the contributing multiplications correct.

1×23	23
2×23	46
5×23	115
10×23	230
20×23	460
50×23	1150
100×23	2300

$$200 \times 23 \quad 4600$$
$$500 \times 23 \quad 11500$$

Work on building the table can stop at this $500 \times$ point, because 11500 is close to the number (11776) we are dividing. This is our estimate. We know the answer will be a little over 500.

To get the accurate answer, all you have to do is a few subtractions, using the multiplication facts from the table and keeping count of how many 23's you have taken away. Keep the layout organised:

```
     11776
    -11500        500      × 23
    ------
       276
      -230         10      × 23
      -----
        46
       -46          2      × 23
       ----        ---
         0         512
```

The answer is   512 $512 \times 23 = 11776$

Try another example ... $3795 \div 23$ ... $? \times 23 = 3795$

A look down the 23x table above shows the answer will be between 100 and 200, closer to 200.

```
      3795
     -2300        100      × 23
     -----
      1495
     -1150         50      × 23
     -----
       345
      -230         10      × 23
      -----
       115
      -115          5      × 23
      -----        ---
         0         165
```

The answer to $? \times 23 = 3795$ is 165.

6 We all Hate Fractions

I have written this chapter to look at two experiences of fractions
1)   the fractions you meet in everyday life
2)   the fractions you meet in school maths

The Fractions you Meet in Everyday Life

The three fractions we meet most often are $\frac{1}{2}$, $\frac{1}{3}$ and $\frac{1}{4}$.

Because these are the 'everyday' fractions they have names
that do not follow the pattern of other fractions, they have their
own unique names
   $\frac{1}{2}$ is named as a half
   $\frac{1}{3}$ is named as a third and
   $\frac{1}{4}$ is named as a quarter

After this the name of the fraction tells you what that fraction
is, for example, $\frac{1}{7}$ is named a seventh, $\frac{1}{20}$ is named a twentieth.

One of the keys to understanding fractions is that the bottom
number has to be treated more as a 'name' than a 'number'.

Size/value

One of the reasons why people do not feel comfortable with fractions is that they contradict their previous experiences of numbers.
For example, in the case of our everyday three fractions:

   $\frac{1}{2}$ is bigger than $\frac{1}{3}$ which, in turn is bigger than $\frac{1}{4}$. Our previous
   sequence of 'bigger' was that 4 is bigger than 3 which, in turn
   is bigger than 2.

The reason for this contradiction is that fractions are about
dividing up quantities. So $\frac{1}{2}$ is what you get when you divide 1 by
2 ... 2 small parts

$\frac{1}{3}$ is what you get when you divide 1 by 3 ... 3 smaller parts

$\frac{1}{4}$ is what you get when you divide 1 by 4 ... 4 even smaller parts.

So with fractions as you get more parts, the parts get smaller.

Think of $\frac{1}{2}$ an hour. This will be a half of 60 minutes ... 30 minutes

Think of $\frac{1}{3}$ an hour. This will be a third of 60 minutes ... 20 minutes

Think of $\frac{1}{4}$ an hour. This will be a quarter of 60 minutes ... 15 minutes

SALES

SALE $\frac{1}{2}$ price everything

TIME

$\frac{1}{4}$ past 7

HAPPY 8 ¾ BIRTHDAY

8 and ¾

The Hidden Divide Sign

The line in the fraction is a hidden divide sign. So

$\frac{1}{7}$ is another way of writing $1 \div 7$

$$\frac{\bullet}{\bullet} \qquad \frac{1}{7}$$

Thus a fraction is about dividing, so the bigger the number that is used to do the dividing then the smaller will be the fraction parts.

So, for example, $\frac{1}{100}$ is much smaller than $\frac{1}{10}$.

Fractions have two numbers, a top number and a bottom number.

The bottom number tells you the name of the fraction, so $\frac{1}{5}$ is a fifth and it tells you that there are 5 parts in the whole. $\frac{1}{9}$ is a ninth and that tells you that there are 9 parts in the whole. The mathematical term for the bottom number is *denominator*. In the middle of this word is *nom*, the French word for name. Denominator is the name of the fraction. The bottom number tells you how many parts the whole has been divided up into and thus how small these parts are.

The top number then tells you how many of these parts you have in that particular fraction. $\frac{3}{7}$ would mean that you have 3 of the 7 parts. $\frac{3}{4}$ means 3 quarters, 3 out of the 4 parts.

The top number may sometimes be bigger than the bottom number, for example, $\frac{3}{2}$ is three halves, or one and a half.

There's more to a half than $\frac{1}{2}$

Half an hour is 30 minutes. We could write this as $\frac{30}{60}$ 30 sixtieths

Half of a £ is 50p. We could write this as $\frac{50}{100}$ 50 hundredths

Half a dozen is 6. We could write this as $\frac{6}{12}$ 6 twelfths

Half a day is 12 hours. We could write this as $\frac{12}{24}$ 12 twenty-fourths

A half can be written as a fraction in many ways, but in every case the top number must be half of the bottom number. $\frac{1}{2}$ is the simplest form of a half. Each of the different ways of writing a half made it into a new 'name', but the relationship between the top and the bottom numbers made each new form still have a value of a 'half'.

The same argument can be made for any fraction. We can change its name, for example, a third $\frac{1}{3}$ could be written as $\frac{8}{24}$ (For example, in 1 day we could work $\frac{8}{24}$ hours, sleep $\frac{8}{24}$ hours and play $\frac{8}{24}$ hours. These 3 thirds make 1 whole day).

Multiplying can make things smaller.

Our previous experience has told us that when we multiply numbers get bigger. This is no longer the case if we are multiplying by a fraction that is less than 1, for example,

$$\frac{1}{2} \times 18 = 9$$
$$\text{or } \frac{1}{4} \times 40 = 10$$

Multiplying by $\frac{1}{2}$ means you divide by 2 and
Multiplying by $\frac{1}{4}$ means that you divide by 4

The number at the bottom of the fraction becomes a divider. Remember that hidden division sign?

If the fraction has a number other than 1 as its top number, then you do multiply by the top number, but you still divide by the bottom number. So now there are two things to do, one is a $\times$ and the other a $\div$

For example $\frac{1}{4}$ of 40 is 10, but
$\frac{3}{4}$ of 40 is first $40 \div 4 = 10$ and then $10 \times 3 = 30$

+ may not always mean add.

I keep returning to the message that fractions are hard because they do things that we haven't met before with other numbers. This happens again when we come to add (and subtract) fractions.

When you add $\frac{1}{2}$ and $\frac{1}{2}$ the + sign only applies to the top number. It helps if you say or speak out loud the 'sum'

'One half plus one half equals two halves.' (and two halves are 1 whole)

$$\frac{1}{2} \quad + \quad \frac{1}{2} \quad = \quad \frac{2}{2}$$

So, we add the top numbers, but we do not add the bottom numbers. This is because the bottom numbers are really 'names' and the top numbers are the quantities of these 'names' that we now can add.

If we were using sevenths, then a subtraction would work like this:

'Three sevenths minus two sevenths leaves (equals) one seventh.'

$$\frac{3}{7} \quad - \quad \frac{2}{7} \quad = \quad \frac{1}{7}$$

We do not subtract the 7's, because that is the name of the fraction, but we do subtract the 2 from the 3, because those numbers tell us how many of the sevenths we are dealing with.

If we subtracted the 7's we would have zero as the bottom number and the fractions would have disappeared (mathematically!)

More trouble with the bottom numbers

This next example is wrong $\frac{1}{2} \quad + \quad \frac{1}{4} \quad = \quad \frac{2}{6}$ ✗

Now we are trying to add two fractions that have different names. We know from our experience of time that half an hour plus a quarter of an hour makes three quarters of an hour, so $\frac{2}{6}$ cannot be correct answer. Once again our previous experience lets us down when we come to work with fractions.

We can only add or subtract fractions when they have the same name, so our wrong example can be done correctly if we consider the half, not as $\frac{1}{2}$ but as two quarters, $\frac{2}{4}$. Then we are adding quarters to quarters

$$\frac{2}{4} \quad + \quad \frac{1}{4} \quad = \quad \frac{3}{4}$$

We can only add or subtract fractions when the have the same name, the same de*nom*inator. If they do not have the same name then one of the fractions, or sometimes both of the fractions, has to be renamed before we add or subtract.

The most reliable (though not always the most efficient) way of adding and subtracting fractions is to always rename both fractions. To do this we use the 'two for the price of one' times tables facts rule, that is

for example $3 \times 4 = 4 \times 3$ and $7 \times 6 = 6 \times 7$

So,

$$\frac{3}{4} - \frac{2}{3} = \frac{3 \times 3}{4 \times 3} - \frac{2 \times 4}{3 \times 4} = \frac{9}{12} - \frac{8}{12} = \frac{1}{12}$$

We multiplied the $\frac{3}{4}$ by $\frac{3}{3}$ and we multiplied the $\frac{2}{3}$ by $\frac{4}{4}$

In this example we shall use the 'two for the price of one' fact $7 \times 6 = 6 \times 7$

$$\frac{3}{7} + \frac{5}{6} = \frac{3 \times 6}{7 \times 6} + \frac{5 \times 7}{6 \times 7} = \frac{18}{42} + \frac{35}{42} = \frac{53}{42}$$

Dividing by fractions

If you remember, we learned that multiplying by a fraction (if it is less than 1) made things smaller. It should not be, therefore, a surprise if I tell you that when we divide by a fraction which is less than 1, the answer is bigger.

For example,

$$5 \div \tfrac{1}{4} = 20$$

As is often the case with fractions, if you talk this through it makes sense. You just have to pick the right words for the 'talking through'

'Divide by 7' can also be expressed as 'how many 7's in?'

So '5 divided by a quarter' can also be expressed as 'How many quarters in 5?'

There are 4 quarters in 1, so
  there are 8 quarters in 2,
      and 12 quarters in 3,
      and 16 quarters in 4 and
      and 20 quarters in 5.

7   Decimal fractions

All the numbers below include a 'decimal'.

   12.5   66.9   0.95   3.25   12.735   and even   £25.95

Decimal fractions are another way of writing numbers less than one. In each of the examples above the figures written after the decimal point (the dot) represent numbers less than one, for example the .5 in 12.5 represents a half. The identifying characteristic is the point, called the 'decimal point.' This decimal point separates the whole numbers from the part numbers.

The most familiar use of decimals is money, where we have whole numbers (pounds) and decimal numbers (pence). Money is a good example for decimals because we divide £1 into ten ten pence coins (each 10p is $\frac{1}{10}$ of £1) and 100 one pence coins (each 1p coin is $\frac{1}{100}$ of £1).

28	.	756
whole numbers	decimal point	part numbers

£54	.	65
whole pounds	decimal point	pence (parts of pounds)

Although decimal fractions do a similar job to ordinary fractions in that they represent numbers less than one, they are more restricted in the values they offer. Decimal fractions only use tenths ($\frac{1}{10}$), hundredths ($\frac{1}{100}$), thousandths ($\frac{1}{1000}$) etc. Like whole numbers (which work on tens, hundreds, thousands, etc), decimal fractions use place value (see page*). The place that a digit holds in the decimal fraction dictates its value. Basically, the place of a digit in the number tells you whether its fraction value is tenths, hundredths, thousandths and so on.

The clue to the ranking of decimals in tens, hundredths and

thousandths and so on is *dec*. Dec means 10 as most often used in *decade*, a 10 year period.

The place value order of decimals is logical. Decimal fractions become ten times smaller each one move right from the decimal point.

For example, 28.756

2	8	.	7	5	6
two	eight	decimal point	seven	five	six
tens	units	decimal point	tenths	hundredths	thousandths
10's	1's		$\frac{1}{10}$'s	$\frac{1}{100}$'s	$\frac{1}{1\,000}$'s

Money

Money is an everyday example of decimals. Sometimes a dash is used instead of the decimal point, but the principle is the same. The pound is the one unit, one whole. Pence are hundredths (since 100 pence make £1) and each ten pence is a tenth (since 10 ten pence coins make £1).

£9.99

£19.95

£4.00

A price is a good example of decimal fractions, though most people do not analyse money in this way, for example £23.95

£	2	3	.	9	5

Two tens three units decimal point nine tenths five hundredths

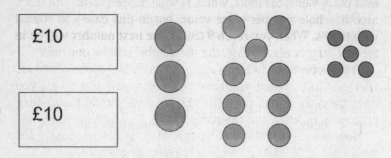

The decimal part of £23.95, that is .95 is shown as 9 ten pence coins and 5 one pence coins. It could also be thought of using just one pence coins, which are each $\frac{1}{100}$ of £1. So .95 could also be shown as 95 one pence coins.

The .95 is $\frac{95}{100}$ of £1 or $\frac{9}{10}$ plus $\frac{5}{100}$ of £1.

Money is useful to show the connection between key fractions and key decimals.

fraction	money	decimal
1	£1 = £1.00	1.00
$\frac{1}{2}$	50p = £0.50	0.50
$\frac{1}{4}$	25p = £0.25	0.25
$\frac{1}{5}$	20p = £0.20	0.20
$\frac{1}{10}$	10p = £0.10	0.10
$\frac{1}{100}$	1p = £0.01	0.01

Counting in decimals

It can help your understanding of decimals if you start by doing a little selected counting in decimals.

Start by counting in tenths,

0.1, 0.2, 0.3, 0.4, 0.5, 0.6, 0.7, 0.8, 0.9 … what is the next number?

The next number is 1.0 (not 0.10). You have moved into the next place value, the units, which is what happens after you reach nine in whole number place value, but in this case you started with tenths. When you reach 9 tenths, the next number will be in the next bigger place value, the 'ten tenths' will be one unit.

Try this counting in tenths again, but with 10p coins, which are £0.1 or £0.10. When you have counted to ten 10p coins, you trade them for pound coin. (Remember how we did that trading process in addition and subtraction?)

Now count in hundredths. Start at 0.01, 0.02, 0.03, 0.04, 0.05, 0.06, 0.07, 0.08, 0.09 ... what is the next number?

The next number is 0.10. Now you are counting in hundredths. When you reach 9 hundredths, the next number will be ten hundredths which is one tenth and takes you to the next place value, that is tenths.

Try this counting in hundredths again, but with 1p coins, which are £0.01, one hundredth of a £1. When you have counted ten 1p coins, you trade them for a 10p coin. 'Trading' should help you to understand the place value system for decimal numbers.

Adding and subtracting decimal numbers

The first step with adding or subtracting decimal numbers is to write them as a 'column' of numbers and *line up the decimal points*, for example with a sum such as:

$$12.3 + 3.219 + 4.35$$

the lining up gives

$$
\begin{array}{r}
12.3 \\
3.129 \\
6074.35 \\
\hline
6089.779
\end{array}
$$

This makes sure that you line up numbers with the same place values, just as you would with whole numbers. Here the decimal point gives you an extra guide for the correct lining up.

In the example chosen, the 2 in 12.3 is 2 units, the 3 in 3.219

is 3 units and the 4 in 6074.35 is 4 units, so these are all lined up to make sure you add like to like.

This also applies to money, for example, £12 plus £3.50 is added as

$$\begin{array}{r} £12.00 \\ £\ 3.50 \\ \hline £15.50 \end{array}$$

Note that £12 is now written as a decimal number £12.00. You line up the £3 with the £2 as they are both unit values of pounds.

The most common mistake when adding decimal numbers is to line them up as though they were whole numbers so 15.4 + 3 is wrongly added as

$$\begin{array}{r} 15.4 \\ 3 \\ \hline 15.7 \end{array}$$ which is WRONG ✗

If you write this as money, the error is obvious

$$\begin{array}{r} £15.4 \\ +£\ 3 \\ \hline £15.7 \end{array}$$ You know from experience that adding together 4p and £3 does not result in £7 or 7p.

Multiplying by decimal numbers

Let's start with an example. Look carefully at the answer.

$$16 \times 0.2 = 3.2$$

When you multiply by a decimal number which is less than one, the answer will be smaller, just as in fraction work. So in the example above 16 becomes 3.2.

There is a rule to help you place the decimal point in the correct place in the answer. First multiply the numbers as though there were no decimal point

$$16 \times 2 = 32$$

now look at the digits on the fraction side of the decimal point. In this case there is *one* digit in 0.2, the 2. The decimal point in the answer is placed at *one* digit in from the right

$$3.2$$

to give an answer of 3.2

In the sum 1.3×0.6, first multiply the numbers, without using any decimals

$$13 \times 6 = 78$$

Now count the 'decimal' digits. There are two, the 3 in 1.3 and the 6 in 0.6, so the decimal point goes in after counting two digits in from the right

$$.78$$

to give an answer of 0.78

It can help to check against basic estimation guide lines:

If the multiplier is less than one, the answer will be smaller, for example:

$$7 \times 0.5 = 3.5$$

If the multiplier is 1, the answer will be the same:

$$7 \times 1.0 = 7.0$$

If the multiplier is bigger than one the answer will be bigger:

$$7 \times 3 = 21$$

As a quick, very rough check, ask the question,

Is the answer smaller, bigger or the same?

Multiplying and dividing by 10, 100, 100 etc

When we multiply decimals by 10 or powers of 10 the same rule applies as when we multiplied whole numbers by 10, 100, 1000 etc. This means if we multiply a unit digit by 10 it moves to have a tens place value. With decimals we can use the decimal point as an extra check.

Look at these examples:

$$3.196 \times 10 = 31.96$$
$$3.196 \times 100 = 319.6$$
$$3.196 \times 1000 = 3196$$

You can focus on the change in value of the 3 each time, or you can look at where the decimal point is in each answer. (It comes after the 6 in the last example).

Since division is the opposite of multiplication, we should expect the reverse to happen when we divide by 10, 100, 1000, etc

$$3196 \div 10 = 319.6$$
$$3196 \div 100 = 31.96$$
$$3196 \div 1000 = 3.196$$

Again you can look at the change in place value of the 3 or at the position of the decimal point in each answer.

Shopping

The favourite decimals used in shops are 0.90, 0.99 and 0.95. Think how many times you have seen prices like £4.99, £19.95 and (under £100!) £99.99.

It really is a great trick, and a fairly international one at that. Shoppers see £14.99 and focus on it as fourteen pounds. The 99 pence is as much as the shop can add to £14 before it moves to £15. It has the benefit of shoppers seeing £14, yet paying virtually £15!

I like those advertisements that say 'A PC for under £500' and the price is £499.99.

When you get to big items like cars and houses, this place value subterfuge is still used. Cars are priced at values like £9 950 and £12 985. Houses at £189 950 and £299 500. A little knowledge of place value in numbers combined with realistic cynicism can be useful.

I feel that this pricing device is aimed (though I think shops do it unconsciously) at inchworms who tend not to scan along the whole number, but instead focus on the first digits. Also they see numbers exactly as written rather than rounded up or down to some more convenient value. I suspect grasshoppers are immune to this pricing strategy.

8 Percentages and Interest

A lot of financial information is presented as percentages, for example the interest rate for a credit card or the savings advertised for a sale in a shop. If we are to understand what sales, loans or saving rates are about we should make an effort to understand percentages.

There are other examples of percentages, too. A recent survey from the web gave some percentages for what people do to recover when a relationship ends:

15% go shopping
22% go drinking
10% go on holiday
36% find a new relationship

Percentages are most frequently, but not exclusively, used for parts of a whole. Comparisons between different percentages are easier to understand than comparisons between different fractions. Percentages are simply ranked as are ordinary numbers, for example 10% is twice 5% or 7.6% is greater than 7.5%.

The key syllables in the word percentage are *cent* which means 100 and *per* which means divide. Percentage is about dividing up into hundredths and is therefore closely related to fractions, but focused on one particular fraction, that is hundredths, $\frac{1}{100}$ and therefore closely related to decimals, too.

So, 50%, fifty percent means $\frac{50}{100}$ or $\frac{1}{2}$

25%, twentyfive percent means $\frac{25}{100}$ or $\frac{1}{4}$

10%, ten percent means $\frac{10}{100}$ or $\frac{1}{10}$

1%, one percent means $\frac{1}{100}$

100% represents 1 (whole). 0% represents 0 (zero). Any percentage value between 0 and 100 represents a fraction, a part of 1.

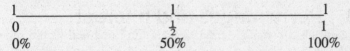

To work out good estimates of fractions and many accurate values too, it helps to be able to divide by 100, by 10, by 2 and to be able to multiply by 2.

Once again we are back to the key numbers, 1, 2, 5, 10 and 100 and once again they will be enough to do many of the calculations needed for percentages.

10%. A special case

It is a recurring theme in this book that maths ideas and facts keep reappearing, often in different disguises. 10% is a good example of this. The quick way to calculate 10% of something is to divide by 10. Being able to divide by 10 is a basic, easy and essential skill, but you may still need to refresh your memory every once in a while.

Reminding you how to divide by 10 …

When you divide a number by one it stays the same value and (with the exception of a special case used in fractions) looks the same. This is not the case when you divide by 10. When you divide a number by ten (one ten) the number looks virtually the same, *but there is an important difference*, the figures/digits in the result are the same and in the same order, but they now have different place values. For example:

$$1\ 234\ 567\ 890 \div 10 = 123\ 456\ 789$$

Each figure now has a place value worth $\frac{1}{10}$ of its previous value (for example, the 7 has moved from being 7000 to 700). This makes sense, since if you divide a number by 10, then all parts of the number should get 10 times smaller!

The last example had a convenient 0 in the units place. If another figure was in the units place, then dividing by 10 takes the answer into decimals, for example

$$98\ 765 \div 10 = 9\ 876.5$$

Again the figures in the answer are the same and in the same order as the original number and, again, each figure in the answer now has a place value which is $\frac{1}{10}$ of its previous value. For example, the 9 was 90 000 and has become 9 000 and 5 units have become .5 (5 tenths). This is a good way to start the calculation. Focus on one digit/figure and make sure its place value goes down to $\frac{1}{10}$ of its previous place value. Then make sure that all the other figures are in the same order as the original number. This will make all these other figures also $\frac{1}{10}$ of their original value. AND don't forget you will find the unit figures (other than 0) becoming decimal figures.

The same principle applies to dividing by 100, one hundred. This will take figures down two place values (there is a reminder built in to the numbers here, 10 has one 0 and the figures move one place, 100 has two 0's and the figures move two places). This two place move makes sense if you start with a simple example, say $400 \div 100 = 4$. The 4 has moved down two place values.

In a harder division such as $456\ 700 \div 100 = 4567$ the same two place value move has occurred. You can check by focussing on the hundreds figure, **7**, which has become a units figure in the answer.

If the number to be divided doesn't have a convenient supply of zeros at the end, you will have an answer which moves into decimal place values.

$$456\ 789 \div 100 = 4567.89$$

Again if you focus on that hundreds figure, the 7, it has again moved to the units place value.

This pattern and these strategies apply to any division further in the 10's series, 1000, 10 000, 100 000, 1 000 000 and so on. To check, focus on an obvious figure whenever possible. For example when dividing by 1000's check that the thousands figure moves down to the units place (1000 is one thousand. 1000 has three zeros, hence a move of three place values).

To work out 1%, divide by 100.
For example, 1% of £750 is £7.50
To work out 10% divide by 10.
For example, 10% of £750 is £75.00
To work out 50% divide by 2.
For example, 50% of £750 is £375.

Once you have worked out these three key values you can use them to work out other values, for example:

2% double the 1% value (multiply the 1% value by 2)
5% half the 10% value (divide the 10% value by 2)
15% add the 10% value and the 5% value
20% double the 10% value
25% half the 50% value
60% add the 50% value and the 10% value
75% add the 50% value and the 25% value

Obviously you can combine these values in other ways to access many other values, for example, for 19% take the 1% value from the 20% value.

An example will show how these key percentage values can work:

Our local travel agent adds 2% to your holiday bill if you pay by credit card. What is the extra payable on a holiday costing £750?

1% is $\frac{1}{100}$, so to work out 1% divide by 100.
£750 ÷ 100 = £7.50
A 2% surcharge will be twice as much, 2 × £7.50
The 2% surcharge is £15.00

Another way to approach this percentage calculation is to interpret 1% as meaning 1 in every 100. Other examples of this approach would be such as interpreting 3% as 3 in every 100, and 20% is interpreted as 20 in every 100 and so on.

Using this interpretation for the travel bill percentage:

1% of £750 is £1 in every £100. There are 7 and $\frac{1}{2}$ hundreds, so a 1% surcharge must be seven and a half pounds, £7.50.

You can use the key values of 1%, 10%, 50% to get other accurate values. You can also use them for close approximations for many other percent values. Once again you make use of the relationships between our key numbers, for example:

5% is half of 10%

So if you can work out 10% of a number, if you then half that 10%, you have the 5% value, as in

£800 ... 10% of £800 is one tenth of 800, that is 800 divided by 10

£800 ÷ 10 = £80.   £80 is 10% of £800,
so 5% of £800 must be half of this £80,
that is £80 0 2 = £40.

20% is twice 10%

If you can work out 10% of a number, it is easy to double the value to get 20%, as in

£800 ... 10% of £800 is one tenth of 800, that is £800 divided by 10

£800 ÷ 10 = £80   £80 is 10% of £800
so 20% of £800 must be twice this £80
that is 2 × £80 = £160.

As a second example, work out 4.5% of £842

10% is £842 ÷ 10 = £84.20
5% is £84.2 ÷ 2 = £42.10
0.5% is the 5% value divided by 10, £42.10 ÷ 10 = £4.21

We could also use the 5% value as our first estimate of the answer.

Now we have used our key values to work out 5% and 0.5%
we can calculate the answer

4.5% is 5% – 0.5%   £42.10
                   – £4.21
                   ───────
                    £37.89

**When newspapers talk about interest rates that have
changed by a 'quarter point' they mean by $\frac{1}{4}$% (0.25%).
To work out this amount, first divide by 100, then divide
by 4 (or by 2 twice).**

VAT, Value Added Tax

When we buy goods in shops, VAT is normally already included
into the price. As I write this book, the VAT rate is 17.5% but who
knows what the future will bring?

Quite often the bills we pay, say to a builder or a plumber or a
telephone bill, do not have VAT added until the end of the bill.

To work out 17.5%:

If you are not using a calculator, then work out the key value
of 10% by dividing by 10.

Double this 10% value to get a (high) estimate of 20%, or, for
an accurate answer:

Use the 10% value and half it to get a 5% value,
then half the 5% to get a 2.5% value.
Add the values for 10% + 5% + 2.5% to get 17.5%

For example, to work out VAT on £244

Start with 10% by dividing by 10   £24.40
5% will be half of the 10% amount   £12.20
2.5% will be half of the 5% amount   £ 6.10

10% + 5% + 2.5%   £42.70

So, 17.5% of £244 is £42.70
And the total cost is now £244.00 + £42.70 = £286.70

If you want to use a calculator to work out this calculation, then you can go quickly to the total cost by using 117.5%

Key in   244
Key in   ×
Key in   117.5
Key in   %

Tipping

Yet again, we return to the key numbers. This particular calculation does not have to be precise. You can round up or down at any stage to make the calculation easier (and depending on how generous you feel about the service you received!)

A 10% tip is calculated by dividing the total value of the bill by 10.

A 15% tip is a two step calculation. Work out the 10% value, then halve this 10% value to get the 5% value and add the two together.

A 12.5% tip is half of a 25% tip, so the calculation is done in three steps, each one dividing by 2. To make this easier, you can round off any of the values.

For example 12.5% of £58.48

Round down and divide by 2
£58 ÷ 2 = £29 or round up £60 ÷ 2 = £30

Round up and divide by 2 £30 ÷ 2 = £15

Divide by 2 £15 ÷ 2 = £7.50

Mortgages

Mortgages are taken out for a long repayment time and usually at a sensible rate of interest, but the total cost of a mortgage can be quite a surprise. For example a mortgage for £100 000 at 6% interest over 25 years will result in a total paid back of over £193 000.

Beware Big Percentages: Store Credit Cards

Some stores issue their own credit cards or offer you a loan from their own finance company. You need to look very carefully at the percentage interest rate charged. This may be close to 30%. If you made no repayments, then in less than 3 years you would owe more than twice the amount you borrowed!

I also compare these extraordinarily high interest rates with what is offered for savings accounts, where you would be lucky (in 2007) to get above 5.5%.

And just imagine the damage to your income if you were tempted by a loan company that charged 170% interest as was revealed in a newspaper article this year.

Other percentage calculations

Type 1. These are questions that ask you to calculate an exact percentage of a number. For example:

What is 35% of £660?

If you chose to use a calculator for this problem, you need to remember the maths meaning of the word 'of' as in 35% **of** £660. It means 'times' or 'multiply'.

So the calculator sequence is:

1) key in 660
2) key in ×
3) key in 35
4) key in %

The sequence follows the maths equation $660 \times 35\% = 231$. The percent (%) key divides by 100 and automatically does the equal (=) key so that the answer comes straight up on the screen. It does two keys for the price of one!

The full maths formula for percentages requires you to know that 'of' means 'multiply' and that % means '$\frac{1}{100}$' or 'divide by 100'

35% of £660 translates into:

$$35 \times 660 \div 100$$

The answer is 231

As a formula (see Chapter 16 for more on algebra):
If we have to calculate p% of £A then the formula is

$$p \times A \div 100$$

Another example of percentages. This one is about VAT.
A builder's estimate for repairing a roof is £1220+ VAT. What is the total amount to pay?

There are two options here. One is to work out 17.5% (VAT rate) of £1220 and add this to £1220. The other is to work out 100% + 17.5% = 117.5% of £1220, which will take you straight to the total bill.

Let's try the second option:
Rephrase the question. What is 117.5 % of £1220? The 'of' means 'multiply' and '%' means 'divide by 100'.

The formula is £1220 × 117.5 ÷ 100

On a calculator, the sequence of keys uses the % button, which automatically divides by 100:

1) key in 1220
2) key in ×
3) key in 117.5
4) key in %

Answer £1433.50

The same strategy can be used with discounts. For example:

A car dealer offers a special summer discount of 12% on a second hand car priced at £6495. How much is the discount price?

A 12% discount means the new price will be 100% – 12%, that is 88% of the original price. The new price is 88% of £6495, so get the calculator and look out for an answer a little less than £6495 (for your estimate work on 10% less).

1) key in 6495
2) key in × (for the 'of')
3) key in 88
4) key in %

The answer is £5715.60

Type 2. These are the questions which ask you to calculate a percentage from two numbers. For example:
A pupil scores 47 marks in an examination where full marks are 80. What is her percent score?

Often with a word problem (on any topic), it is a good idea to read and then reword the question until it takes a form that makes sense to you. For this question, you could rephrase the pupil's score to be, '47 out of 80.' The words 'out of' make the question a fraction $\frac{47}{80}$, which means 47 divided by 80. To make the fraction a percent, multiply by 100:

$$\frac{47}{80} \times 100 = 58.75\%$$

Alternatively, once you have decided this is a $\frac{47}{80}$ question and thus identified the question as a division, you can use the % key on the calculator. There are four steps:

1) key in 47
2) key in ÷
3) key in 80
4) key in %.

(This time the % button automatically multiplies by 100 and also activates the = key).

The sequence of keys in these percentage calculations follows the formula, as for example with $\frac{47}{80} \times 100$

The formula is $\dfrac{A}{B} \times 100$ or $A \div B \times 100$

9 Interconverting Fractions, Decimals and Percentages

Sometimes you have to convert a fraction to a percentage or a fraction to a decimal or some other interchange between the three. Since decimals, percentages and fractions are all ways of representing quantities that are less than a whole number, it seems logical that they should be interlinked. They are.

Additionally, it will help you to understand the three separate topics if you see how closely they are related.

The best way to understand the links is to remember how each is constructed. This may mean a re-read of the relevant chapters.

As ever, start by focusing on some key values

fraction	decimal	percentage
$\frac{1}{2}$	0.50	50
$\frac{1}{10}$	0.10	10
$\frac{1}{100}$	0.01	1

The decimal to percentage and the percentage to decimal links are the most obvious numerically. The digits are the same, for example 0.50 and 50%. There is a little more involved with interchanges involving fractions, but this is not an insurmountable problem.

First, let's look at the key values to demonstrate how the translations are done.

$\frac{1}{2}$, 0.50 and 50% all represent the same value, a half. If you understand the maths used in each of these representations of a half, it becomes quite obvious that they are the same. Look at these three interpretations of the maths code used here;

$\frac{1}{2}$ means $1 \div 2$ which divides out as 0.50

$\frac{1}{2}$ can also be written as $\frac{50}{100}$ (see page 82)

50% means $\frac{50}{100}$ (see page 94)

0.50 means 50 hundredths, which is also $\frac{50}{100}$ (see page 94)

We can now extend these key values into other values by combining and by using the procedures we have used in other chapters, for example, dividing by 2 twice

$$\frac{1}{2} \div 2 = \frac{1}{4} \qquad 0.50 \div 2 = 0.25$$

Now divide both the $\frac{1}{4}$ and 0.25 by 2 (which is dividing by 2 for a third time)

$$\frac{1}{4} \div 2 = \frac{1}{8} \qquad 0.25 \div 2 = 0.125$$
$$\frac{1}{8} \text{ is } 0.125$$

We can also extend our key facts by doubling:

$$10\% \text{ is } 0.10$$

double both these

$$10\% \times 2 = 20\% \qquad 0.10 \times 2 = 0.20$$
$$20\% \text{ is } 0.20$$

We can also extend our key values by combining them:

$$0.50 \text{ is } 50\%$$
$$0.25 \text{ is } 25\%$$

Combine these by addition

$$0.75 \text{ is } 75\%$$

(If you are combining fractions you will have to remember the rules for adding and subtracting fractions, see pages 83-85)

Interchanging by formulas

This relies on an understanding of the codes involved in fractions, decimals and percentages. Although the three are written differently, they all have the same basic idea.

Fractions include a hidden division sign, for example $\frac{1}{4}$ is $1 \div 4$.

Decimals and percentages can be converted to fractions (hundredths), which means they then also include a division.

For example:

0.25 is 25 hundredths, $\frac{25}{100}$, that is $25 \div 100$ and

25% is 25 percent, 25 out of 100, $\frac{25}{100}$, which is $25 \div 100$

The conversions are centred on division and multiplication

use hundredths		divide by 100
eg. 0.50 is $\frac{50}{100}$ is $\frac{1}{2}$		eg 50% is $\frac{50}{100}$ is 0.50
FRACTION	**DECIMAL**	**PERCENTAGE**
do the division		multiply by 100
eg. $\frac{1}{2}$ is $1 \div 2$ is	0.50 and 0.50	$\times 100$ is 50%

10 Measuring: It's all Greek words to me: deci, centi, milli, kilo and Mega.

I am sure that most people would rather avoid fractions of any kind. This is one of the reasons we have pence rather than 'one hundredths of a pound'. Even though we write prices as a decimal, for example £15.75, we understand and interpret that price as 'fifteen pounds and seventy five pence' rather than 'fifteen point seven five pounds'.

We have a system for avoiding the use of decimals in our measurements of length, weight and volume. The metric system uses prefixes to tell us when something is a tenth or a hundredth or a thousandth instead of using a decimal point (or a fraction). The prefixes are: deci ($\frac{1}{10}$), centi ($\frac{1}{100}$), milli ($\frac{1}{1000}$) and micro ($\frac{1}{1\,000\,000}$)

There are also prefixes for telling us about big quantities, too.
These prefixes are: kilo (1000×) and Mega (1 000 000×)
When it comes to measuring things, we use specific units;
for length we use *metres*
for weight (mass) we use *kilograms* and
for volume we use *litres*.

As with the £, these units are not perfect for every occasion, so with pounds we have to use pence, and with these units we use sub-units or multiple units which are based on 10 and powers of 10 (again).

Metres, litres and kilograms are all part of a metric system, a system that works in multiples of 10 and divisors of 10 (as with decimals), just like our everyday number system. The metric system has a set of prefixes which can be added to the front of a unit to tell us what decimal or what multiplier we are using. So, the metric system allows us to avoid fractions and decimals by using a prefix instead.

For example, when using metres, if we want to talk about a smaller length we might use *milli*metres. The pre-fix 'milli' always means $\frac{1}{1000}$, one thousandth.

We might use *centi*metre instead. As you may have guessed from previous experiences of *cent*, this relates to a hundred. This time to $\frac{1}{100}$, one hundredth.

If we want to talk about bigger lengths
we use *kilo*metres, which means 1000 metres

The metric system is based on ten and powers of ten (10, 100, 1 000, etc). The fraction prefixes used are, therefore, not surprisingly, related to the decimal fractions ($\frac{1}{10}$, $\frac{1}{100}$, $\frac{1}{1000}$, etc).

The prefixes used for less than 1 are:

deci, d (not used a lot), $\frac{1}{10}$

centi, c, $\frac{1}{100}$ and

milli, m, $\frac{100}{1000}$

micro, μ, $\frac{1}{1\,000\,000}$

The table shows how this is done for metres.

$\frac{1}{10}$ metre 0.1 metre 1 decimetre 1dm

$\frac{1}{100}$ metre 0.01 metre 1 centimetre 1cm

$\frac{1}{1000}$ metre 0.001 metre 1 millimetre 1mm

$\frac{1}{1\,000\,000}$ metre 0.000 000 1 metre 1 micrometre 1Bm

The prefixes are an alternate way of writing a fraction or a decimal. Instead of writing $\frac{59}{100}$ metre or 0.59 metre, we write 59 cm (or 590 mm). Instead of writing $\frac{734}{1000}$ metre, or 0.734 metre, we write 734 mm.

Builders and DIY stores are more likely to use mm rather than cm for fractions of a metre, for example

20mm is $\frac{20}{1000}$ metre, which is $\frac{2}{100}$ metre
100mm is $\frac{100}{1000}$ metre, which is $\frac{1}{10}$ metre
1500mm is $\frac{100}{1000}$ metre, which is 1.5 or $1\frac{1}{2}$ metre.

For big distances we have to use a prefix that means '1000x', *kilo*.

A metre is approximately one long stride, but it is still not a big distance in terms of say, travelling from London to York. For these bigger distances we use the kilometre. The prefix, *kilo*, which has been added to metre, means one thousand of. A kilometre is 1000m and is shortened to 1 km.

Miles and Kilometres

1 mile = 1.6093 km   1 mile = 1.6 km or use $\frac{8}{5}$ km
1 km = 0.6214 miles 1 km = 0.6 mile or use $\frac{6}{10}$ mile

So to convert kilometres to miles you can either multiply by 6 and divide by 10 or multiply by 5 and divide by 8. (The accurate answer is about half way between these two estimates)

To convert miles to kilometres you do the opposite, that is

Multiply by 10 and divide by 6, or

Multiply by 8 and divide by 5.

This is a good example of using the check question 'Is the answer bigger or smaller?'

Miles are longer than kilometres, so a set number of miles will be converted to a bigger number of kilometres.

Kilometres are shorter than miles, so a set number of kilometres will be converted to a smaller number of miles.

For example, to convert 240 km into miles.

The answer will be a smaller number (because miles are bigger than kilometres). The key (approximate) values are

10 km = 6 miles
or 8 km = 5 miles

So choose the key value which fits the numbers you have the best. for 240 km the 8 km = 5 miles is good.

Now develop the key value, using simple multiples, starting with 10×.

80 km = 50 miles
160 km = 100 miles
240 km = 150 miles

This can also be used for mph and kph conversions. Remember

that a kph value will be bigger (as a number) than its mph equivalent, for example 50kph is approximately 30mph and 120 kph is approximately 70 mph.

Measuring volume in metric units (volume is sometimes called capacity).

The basic unit of volume in the metric system is the litre, shortened to l. A litre is quite a large volume (about $1\frac{3}{4}$ pints) so again prefixes are used to deal with smaller volumes.

The prefixes in the metric system are always the same, d for deci, which is $\frac{1}{10}$; c for centi, which is $\frac{1}{100}$ and m for milli, which is $\frac{1}{1000}$. This gives decilitres, dl, centilitres, cl and millilitres, ml.

A can of soft drink is usually 330 ml $\frac{330}{1000}$ litre about $\frac{1}{3}$ litre

A bottle of whisky or any spirit is usually 70 cl $\frac{70}{100}$ litre (or 7dl)

A bottle of wine is usually 75 cl $\frac{75}{100}$ litre 3/4 litre

A tin of gloss paint may be 500 ml $\frac{500}{1000}$ litre $\frac{1}{2}$ litre

A pint of milk is 568 ml $\frac{568}{1000}$ litre just over $\frac{1}{2}$ litre, though milk is often sold in cartons of 1.136 litre which is 2 pints.

I have yet to spot the rational for producers using centilitres for some liquids and millilitres for others. It just confuses most customers.

Measuring weight (mass) in metric units

The basic unit of weight in the metric system is a little different in that it already has a prefix, the *kilo*gram, kg. The prefix kilo means 1000 times. This means that the kilogram is 1000 grams.

A normal bag of sugar is 1 kg, so a gram would be, $\frac{1}{1000}$, one thousandth of the sugar in that bag. A gram is quite a small weight, for example, a drawing pin weighs about a gram.

So, for weights less than a kilogram instead of a prefix the gram, g is used. The prefix is dropped. One gram is $\frac{1}{1000}$ of a kilogram.

A bag of sugar weighs 1 kg

A packet of butter weighs 250 g $\frac{250}{1000}$ kg 1/4 kg

A packet of fudge weighs 100 g $\frac{100}{1000}$ kg 1/10 kg

Big weights. The tonne.

Once again weight is a little different to other metric units. A thousand kilograms should be a Megagram, because the Mega prefix means

1 000 000, one million. A million is one thousand thousands (hence we use Megastar to mean someone pretty famous).

For the rather individual situation for weight, one thousand kilograms is called a *tonne*.

1 tonne is 1000 kilograms

In the 'old' UK system of measures we used a *ton*, which is 2240 lb (pounds).

By chance, 1 ton and 1 tonne are actually very close in value.

11 Probability. Understanding the Odds in Life

This is an application of fractions, decimals and percentages used, among others, by gamblers and insurance actuaries. It puts the probability of any event or occurrence on a scale between 0 and 1.

A probability of 0 means that the occurrence is impossible.

A probability of 1 means that the occurrence is certain.

Not surprisingly, then, a probability of $\frac{1}{2}$ (or 0.5) is a 'fifty-fifty' or evens chance, the most common example of which is tossing a coin and choosing heads or tails. Probabilities can also be expressed as fractions or percentages.

The probability line.

0	$\frac{1}{2}$	1
I_____	I_____	I
impossible	evens	certain
0	0.5	1
0	50%	100%

Poker gets a lot of publicity these days. The best 'hand' in poker will take us towards the impossible end of the probability line. The odds of getting a royal flush on the first deal, five cards of the same suit, 10, jack, queen, king and ace are 1 in 650,000 or 0.0000015

The chance of winning the Lottery with one entry is around 14 million to 1 or $\frac{1}{14\,000\,000}$, which is a number even closer to 0!

When probabilities are given as percentages, the usual 'translation' applies, so a probability of 1 becomes 100% and $\frac{1}{2}$

becomes 50%. Weather forecasters sometimes use percentages to indicate the relative probability of rain or snow. A 90% chance of rain means that rain is very likely. A 10% chance of snow means there will be little chance of building a snowman.

Spinning a coin

Probabilities are about the relationship between a successful outcome and all the possible outcomes. To help understand this, think about spinning a coin and calling 'Heads'.

A coin has two sides. If it is a 'fair' coin, the chance of getting a 'head' or a 'tail' will be the same. This means that there are two equally possible outcomes altogether. If the coins lands as 'heads', this would be the successful outcome. So you have 1 successful outcome. 'Tails' is the other, unsuccessful outcome. So the number of all possible outcomes is 2 and the chance of getting a 'head' on each spin of the coin is 1 out of 2 or $\frac{1}{2}$.

I can write a generalised probability fraction as:

$$\text{Probability} = \frac{\text{the number of successful outcomes}}{\text{the total number of all the outcomes}}$$

('all the outcomes' means adding together the number of successes and the number of failures)

Let's apply this to throwing a six sided die (die is singular for dice). Say you want to get a four. That means you have 1 successful outcome, a four. The die has six sides and six numbers, so there are six possible ways that the die can land. So all the possibilities are 6.

The probability of throwing a four =

$$\frac{\text{The number of successful outcomes}}{\text{The number of all possible outcomes}} = \frac{1}{6}$$

For horse racing, the bookies modify the probability fractions. Odds of 10 to 1 on a horse means that the bookie has judged that the horse has ten chances of losing to one chance of winning. The total number of 'outcomes' is therefore $1 + 10$, so the probability fraction is $\frac{1}{11}$.

Now let's look at the probabilities in the stars ...

I like reading my astrological forecast, but there is a probability barrier preventing me from taking it too seriously. Let me explain.

Say the population of the UK is sixty million. There are twelve star signs. Say that the birthdays of these sixty million people are evenly distributed through the year, then there are about 5 000 000, five million people sharing each star sign.

I figure three probability related things from this:

It is a certainty that all predictions for a star sign will have to be vague!

It is probable that at least one of these five million people with the same star sign will fulfil one of these vague predictions ('exciting news about money will land on your doormat').

I think it is a low probability that descriptions of typical Taureans (or whichever star sign) will fit all the five million Taureans in England (except, of course, the bits I agree with)

But I still read my 'stars'!

12 Cooking, Mixing Concrete and Changing Money Abroad

These three activities are about *proportion*.

Proportion is about keeping the relative contributions of all the ingredients the same no matter how much concrete you mix or how many people you cook for.

Proportion (or ratio) is basically a division process, but with an extra step. We use it, without realising it is a proportion, when cooking, for DIY, for converting money for our holidays abroad and when calculating percentages (Chapter 8)

As a student I was forced by lack of finance, extreme hunger and flat mates who were the culinary equivalent of illiterate to learn how to cook for myself. For the first time, even as the holder of an A level certificate for maths, I appreciated the practical applications of proportion.

Later in my life I became a (mortgaged) house owner. Again lack of finance, crumbling walls, muddy paths and friends who were the DIY equivalent of illiterate forced me to learn how to mix (and use) mortar and concrete. For the second time in my life I appreciated the practical use of proportion.

Both these real life examples of proportion take a rough (approximate) attitude to complete accuracy. But the principle you use is the same as with accurate proportion calculations.

Start with food and cooking. A simple recipe for a crumble topping is:

150g flour
75g butter
75g sugar

150g is twice 75 g, so the proportions (or ratio) are 2 parts of flour, 1 part of butter, 1 part of sugar, which makes a total of 4 parts. The four parts add up (150g + 75g + 75g) to make 300g of crumble topping.

You need to keep to these proportions if you want to make smaller or bigger quantities of crumble. It would be a very dry and non-crumbly crumble if you only doubled the quantity of flour to make more crumble. You need to double the quantity of all the ingredients to make the recipe still work.

When dealing with proportion (or ratios) there are two numerical areas on which to focus:

the individual proportional parts; in this example, 2, 1 and 1

the total number of proportional parts; in this example 2 + 1 + 1 = 4

Although the recipe I used worked with 75g, 75g and 150g, I could use any values in the 1 to 1 to 2 proportions, say 1kg of sugar, 1kg of butter and 2kg of flour (for a very large amount of crumble topping, 1 kg + 1kg + 2kg = 4kg).

So whatever I use to multiply the quantity of one ingredient, I must use the same multiplier for all the quantities. If I double one quantity, I must double all the quantities. If I halve one quantity, I must halve all the quantities.

Now, to move to the concrete experience of proportion (not to be confused with crumble mix, but similar in some respects for my cooking skills).

The proportions (ratio) I used for mixing concrete were by volume not weight. I interpreted 'one volume part' as 'a heaped amount on a shovel', so for a dry mix of concrete the proportion parts are:

1 cement	1 heaped shovel
2 sand	2 heaped shovels
4 aggregate (chippings)	4 heaped shovels

The total number of parts is 1 + 2 + 4 = 7.

So if it takes 35 heaped shovels to almost fill my wheelbarrow, I will need $35 \div 7 = 5$ times each proportion part. I need to multiply each proportion part by 5.

$5 \times 1 = 5$ heaped shovels of cement
$5 \times 2 = 10$ heaped shovels of sand
$5 \times 4 = 20$ heaped shovels of aggregate
Total 35 heaped shovels of concrete

To do this calculation, I needed to know the total number of proportion parts (in this example, 7). I divided the quantity I had to make (35) by this total number of parts to find out how many lots of each part was needed. I needed to divide 35 by 7, $35 \div 7 = 5$, to work out that I needed 5 lots of each proportion part and then I multiplied each proportion part by 5.

Now look at a 'reverse' example, where you have to divide something up into proportions. (Ordinary division divides things up into equal parts. Proportions divide things up into unequal parts. This means that you have to add up all the proportion parts to find the total number of parts before you do the division).

Say a lottery syndicate has five members, Mr Black, Mr White, Mr Orange, Mr Red and Mr Green (not Reservoir Dogs!). Each Saturday, Mr Black pays in £3, Mr White pays in £2, Mr Orange, Mr Red and Mr Green each pay in £1. They agree to share any winnings in the same proportion as their 'investments'.

They win £4000.

The parts for the five men are 3, 2, 1, 1, 1

The total number of parts is $3 + 2 + 1 + 1 + 1 = 8$

The first step is to find out the value of '1 part', so to do this £4000 has first to be divided up into 8 parts

$$£4000 \div 8 = £500$$

So 1 part is £500
2 parts are $2 \times £500 = £1000$
3 parts are $3 \times £500 = £1500$

To summarise (and check)

Mr Orange	£500
Mr Red	£500
Mr Green	£500
Mr White	£1000
Mr Black	£1500
Total	£4000

Three other everyday examples of proportion are maps, plans and architectural models. An artistic example would be a drawing (in the traditional style rather than Picasso) of a human body. It would be obvious if, say the legs were out of proportion to the rest of the body (except with Barbie dolls, but then they are not human) or if the eyes were drawn too high on the head.

Inverse proportion

So far we have looked at direct proportion, for example if you were making crumble mix and you doubled the amount of flour, you would have to double the amounts of the other two ingredients as well. In direct proportion if you half one part you half the other parts, if you multiply one part by ten, then you have to multiply the other parts by ten.

There is also an *inverse proportion*, where, for example doubling one quantity is balanced by halving the other quantity. For example, if you travel along a motorway for 120 miles at a constant 40 miles per hour, you will travel for 3 hours (and annoy a lot of people). If you then do the same journey at twice the speed, 80 miles per hour, your travelling time will be halved to $1\frac{1}{2}$ hour.

A classic example used in schools involves builders building a wall, for example,

If one bricklayer builds a wall in 12 hours, then, providing they work at the same rate and keep out of each others way, three bricklayers will build the same size wall in 4 hours. Using three times the bricklayers gets the job done in one third of the time (in theory, but then much of the 'real life' maths in school text books is very much 'in theory').

If you look at this bricklayer example in terms of the numbers involved, you will see a constant value in multiplying the number of bricklayers by the time taken to build the wall.

number of bricklayers

$$1 \times 12 = 3 \times 4$$

time to build the wall

This is an example of the relative size (value) of the two multipliers for a given product, for example, if the product is 24, the multipliers can be:

1 × 24 = 24
2 × 12 = 24
3 × 8 = 24
4 × 6 = 24
6 × 4 = 24
8 × 3 = 24
12 × 2 = 24
24 × 1 = 24

As the bold numbers get bigger, the plain numbers get correspondingly smaller.

Foreign exchange and proportion

When you travel abroad you have to cope with a different currency with a different value. If you want to convert between the currencies, it is a similar process to working out proportion. For example if you get 80 rupees for £1, you would expect to get twice the number of rupees for £2 and ten times the number of rupees for £10.

In addition to making use of the proportion ideas again, I am going back to the key numbers 1, 2, 5, 10, 20, 50 and 100 once more.

For much of your spending you will probably be happy with an estimate (for example, the true rate of exchange for rupees is 79.26 as I write this). If you are cautious then you may wish to know whether the estimate is high or low.

For example, in December 2006, £1 was equivalent to 19.42 Mexican pesos. (This is an easy rate of exchange, being very close to 20 pesos to £1).

If you know the rate of exchange, then you can work out the cost of meals, shopping, hotels and so forth. This is vital for keeping to budget.

There are accurate ways to calculate the exchange values, but you will need to have a calculator on hand. There are also good estimate ways, which are really a variation of proportion. And they can be a lot quicker than with a calculator.

I set up a short chart of estimated key values and their exchange rates.

Let's look at the estimate method, using some exchange rates that were current in Winter 2006/07. Although these examples are specific, I will try to build up a general method for you to use. The strategy uses proportions involving easy numbers.

So, for Mexico, the key exchange values are £1 = 20 pesos

Pesos	**20**	40	100	200	500	1000
Pounds	**1**	2	5	10	25	50

To work out if the estimates in this chart are over or under, use the 'Is the answer bigger or smaller?' question. If I divide by an exchange rate that is bigger than the true value I will get a smaller answer for £s. So all the estimates in the chart above are low. The actual amount in £s will be higher than on my chart… but not much!

An example where you may need to refine your estimate for higher values is the current value of the Swiss franc. The current exchange rate for Switzerland is 2.31 francs for £1. This can be estimated into numbers which are easier to use, since

$$4 \times 2.31 = 9.24 \text{ francs}$$

which is fairly close to 10 francs, giving a key exchange rate of £4 to 10 francs.

I am using an exchange rate of 2.5 francs to £1, which means my conversions from francs to pounds will be an underestimate (just under 10%)

So, the key proportion is £1 to 4 francs and from this you can build up a mini-chart or table of exchange values. For the higher values, which I have marked with *, because 2.5 is about 10% more than 2.3, I have added on 10% (divide by 10 and add on, for example, first estimate for 50 francs is £20, so divide by 10 to get £2 and add to £20 to get £22)

Francs	2.31	5	**10**	20	*50	*100	*150	*200
Pounds	1	2	**4**	8	22	44	66	88

Because my estimate is less accurate for francs then for pesos, I have constructed a more accurate estimate chart for the conversion from pounds to francs on the principle that, of course, both charts can be used for conversions in either direction.

Pounds	1	2	5	10	15	20	50	100	150	200	500
Francs	2.3	4.6	11.5	23	35	46	110	230	340	460	1100

This second chart is a similar idea to the table used for 'long' division (page 78). It uses patterns like 0, 100, 1000 and combines numbers to make new values (for example 100 + 50 = 150. You do not have to treat each exchange as a separate, unconnected calculation).

From these key exchanges you can work out others, for example, 120 francs is 100 + 20 francs which exchanges at £44 + £8, that is £52. This strategy combines proportion with building up and breaking down numbers.

The exchange rate for US dollars is currently £1 for $1.92. This obviously rounds up to $2.

If you divide a dollar value by 2 to estimate the £ value then you can ask yourself the question '*Is the answer bigger or smaller than the true conversion?*' In other words is your estimated rate for converting dollars to pounds going to give you an answer that is more then the accurate value or an answer that is lower than the accurate answer?

If you divide a price by a number bigger than 1.92 then you will get a smaller answer, so using 2 instead of 1.92 will underestimate the price in £'s. The real price will be higher.

Sweden's kronor is at 13.14 for £1, which comes very close to easy numbers at £3 for 39.42 kronor, rounded to 40 kronor for £3. I use 40 kronor to £3 as my starting value when building up a key value chart.

Kronor	20	**40**	80	100	130	200	400	1000
£	1.50	**3**	6	7.50	10	15	30	75

All you need in your pocket is a small card with the key value and some derived values and you can look like a mental arithmetic foreign exchange wizard.

I think we are conditioned to believe that we should be able to do whole calculations completely in our heads and that charts like these are soft options. We should learn to do what is effective for us. I would argue that for many people these little charts are more effective than calculators for quick estimations of currency values. They certainly provide sensible support for mental calculations.

13 What it Means to be Average

Averages are often used in statistics, probably because they are simple to calculate and because many people think they understand the concept of an 'average'. But, on the principle that you should be very wary when interpreting any statistics, you should be wary when interpreting averages.

First, what are averages and how are they calculated?

An average is usually taken to mean something in the middle or something typical, like an average family. (I selected this example to sow the first seeds of caution in your mind).

In fact three different averages are used in maths. The most common of these is the arithmetic average (also called the 'mean value'). To calculate an arithmetic average you add up all the values and then divide by the number of values you added up.

This can be written as a formula;

Arithmetic average = The sum of all values ÷ The number of values (how many values were used)

Remember the strategy we used for adding a list of numbers? Casting out tens. It is very useful when working out averages.

An example:

In one week in February, the temperatures each day were 12°C, 10°C, 9°C, 6°C, 4°C, 3°C and 5°C. What is the average temperature for the week?

The sum of all the temperatures is; $12 + 10 + 9 + 6 + 4 + 3 + 5 = 49$

The number of values used is 7

Average = $49 ÷ 7 = 7°C$

This is quite a sensible average. All the values were

reasonably similar, so the average was a middle example with not too much of a spread of values (called the range) each side.

The 'range' is worked out by subtracting the smallest value from the biggest value.

In this example, the smallest value is 3 and the biggest is 12, so the range is 9° C.

Averages do not always give a sensible middle measure, as in this next example.

The average salaries of five men in a factory are £10 000, £12 000, £8 000, £15 000 and £200 000. What is the average salary at the factory?

The sum of all the salaries is:

£10 000 + £12 000 + £8 000 + £15 000 + £200 000 = £245 000
The number of salaries is 5
The average salary is 245 000 ÷ 5 = £44 000

The average has been distorted by the one large salary. If the range of values was quoted as well as the average, this would help to make the picture a little clearer. The range is £220 000 − £8 000 = £212 000.

Another less than informative average value is average speed;

A family set off in their car to make a 120 mile journey, mostly along the A 38. The journey takes 4 hours. What is the average speed?

Average speed is calculated by dividing the distance travelled by the time taken

average speed = distance travelled ÷ time taken to travel

Put into the equation (formula) the values from the question:

average speed = 120 miles ÷ 4 hours = 30 mph

If you think about a car journey on non-motorway roads, speed is rarely constant, the cars stop for traffic lights, slow up behind tractors. Children may need to stop for toilets or a drink. The average speed gives only very basic information about the journey.

Treat averages cautiously. They can only tell you some of the information needed towards the whole picture.

50% is sometimes used to indicate the middle value, the average. I often think education officials will only be satisfied with teachers when all children are above average!

14 Angles

Angles are often to do with turning. If you turn through 180 degrees then you turn round to the opposite direction. If you walked around a room, staying close to the walls, at each corner you would turn through 90 degrees. If you walked all around the walls inside the circular dome of St Paul's cathedral in London, you would have turned through 360 degrees.

Sometimes a plane is put 'on hold' while waiting for permission to land. This means it will be circling above the airport. The plane will turn through 360 degrees for each complete circle.

The most familiar angle in everyday life is 90 degrees. We have a symbol for degrees, so we can write 90 degrees more concisely as 90°.

This special angle of 90° is in such common use that its own name, the *right angle*. 90 degrees is the angle in corners of most of our buildings, doors, picture frames, book pages, etc.

90° is also the angle between a vertical line and a horizontal line.

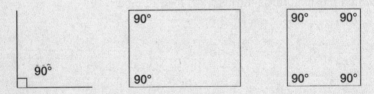

Unfortunately the key angles do not use the easiest numbers. As I have just said, a right angle is 90° when 100° would have been easier to work with numerically. A complete circle is 360°. You have to keep this difference to the tens system (where the key numbers are 1, 10, 100, 1000 and so on) in your mind when you see work involving angles. However, since we have looked at the relationship between 10 and 9 and 100 and 90, it shouldn't be a new experience to use that link yet again.

Some peoples' understanding of angles is blurred because they do not realise that when two lines meet at an angle, the angle size is not dependent on the length of either line (see figure). The length of the meeting lines does not affect the value of any angle. The 90 degree corner is 90° whether it is the corner of a page in a book or the corner of a football field.

The fact that the size of an angle between two lines is completely unaffected by the lengths of those two lines applies to any and all angles.

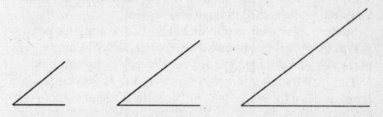

A right angle is a quarter of the angle you would turn through if you turned a complete circle. If you turn through four right angles (4 × 90° = 360°), then you have turned through 360°, which is complete circle.

The hour hand of a clock turns through 360° every 12 hours, which means it turns through 90° every 3 hours.

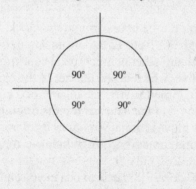

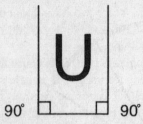

The U turn, immortalised by politicians, is a turn through 180°, or two right angles.

Other angles

The right angle provides your key reference for other angles. For example, 45° is half of 90°

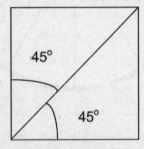

A clock can help you picture 30°. The circular face of a clock means that the second, minute and hour hand all turn through 360° every time they go once around the clock face.

It is usually good to relate topics to show how the same ideas crop up in different disguises. In this case it is clocks, time and angles

If you focus on the 12 hours around the clock, then the hour hand turns through 90° from 12 to 3, from 3 to 6, from 6 to 9 and from 9 to 12 (and any other consecutive 3 hour time). If we pick on the 12 to 3 move, which is one quarter of the clock, it is obvious that the angle turned is 90°, one quarter of a complete turn.

This must mean that the hour hand turns through one third of 90° every time it moves from one hour to the next. For example, when the hour hand turns from 2 to 3, it moves through 30° (one third of 90°)

There is a 30° degree angle between every consecutive hour figures.

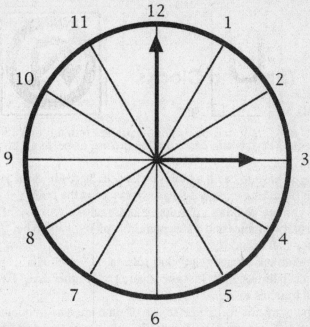

Triangles

A triangle is so called because it has 3 angles. These angles may all be the same size, or have two angles the same size or have all three angles of different sizes.

Whichever of these three possibilities it is, the three angles inside a triangle always add up to 180°

If you wanted to check this 180° rule, then draw any triangle and cut it up to separate the 3 angles (see Fig 14.7). Put the three angles together as shown. They will always make 180° which is a straight line or two right angles.

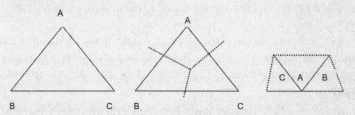

15 Time and Clocks

Time in everyday life can either be precise or be an approximation.

If you have to catch a train you have to be ready at the station at the right time … and if you are lucky so is the train.

If you are walking your dog you are unlikely to say, 'I'll be back in 33 minutes and 47 seconds.' It's more likely to be, 'I'll be about a half hour.'

If you ask someone, 'What time is it?' the usual reply is 'Almost half past.' Or 'Just after quarter to.' Rather than 'Twenty-seven minutes to eight.'

The demands for a precise use of time are less frequent than for approximations in everyday life, so we have less practice and we tend, therefore, to be less skilled at the precise aspect of time.

How is time different to other number work?

When we learn something new we try to relate it to previous experiences and knowledge. Time is another one of those maths topics which does not fit into previous experience, for example, although time uses the usual set of digits 0, 1, 2, 3, 4, 5, 6, 7, 8 and 9, it does have three differences to normal counting.

One is that the clock uses 12 (and 24) hours rather than 10.

The next is that the numbers are arranged in a circle (rather than a line).

This takes us to the third difference. The circle means that the cycle of numbers repeats. You get to 12 and start over again at 1.

Of course a calendar is not circular. It is truly an example of a time line!

A clock (or watch) face gives three quantities of time. There are the 12 numbers round the clock face for the hours. Then there are 60 marks around the clock for the 60 minutes (60 minutes make 1 hour). Those 60 marks also stand for the 60 seconds that make one minute. The clock face acts as three circular number lines, one for hours, one for minutes and one for seconds.

I cannot think of any other number line that does this. Perhaps this unique character of clocks and watches is one of the reasons why people find time difficult.

A digital watch has some advantages. It is easy to 'read' the time on a digital clock. What you see is what you say. For example in the Figure above, the time reads as 7:10.

Unfortunately when people say time it is not always what the digital clock 'says'. For example, a friend may say, 'Ten past seven' which is not giving the numbers in the same order as the digital clock's 7:10, even though both are the same time.

The analogue clock also gives you a visual image of 'time past' and 'time to come'. For example, 'Half past six' makes visual sense on an analogue clock, but has no significant visual image on a digital clock.

'Telling' the Time

As I have just said, telling the time with a digital display is simply a matter of reading the numbers you see. Telling the time from a traditional, analogue clock face is a little less straightforward.

For our start on this topic, it is best to focus on the two main 'hands' of the clock, the hour hand and the minute hand.

The hour hand moves continuously around the clock face, but at a speed that is so slow you will not see it move. Because it moves continuously it will not always be pointing straight to an hour, a number on the clock face. For example, at half past an hour the hour hand will be pointing half way between two numbers.

The minute hand moves sixty times faster, but it is still difficult to see it actually moving. (The second hand moves sixty times faster again, so it is possible to see it moving).

The advantage of a traditional analogue clock face is that it shows the time in the context of the 12 hours on the face. It gives a visual image of what time has gone by and how much is left. We can see where the hour hand and the minute hand are around the circle that is the clock face. For example at 4 o'clock (Fig 15.1), we can see that relative to 12 noon, four hours have past and that there are 8 hours to go until 12 midnight. The clock face shows that time in the sense of $\frac{1}{3}$ of the circle has gone and $\frac{2}{3}$ are left to go, because the hour hand is pointing at 4.

The same is true for the minute hand. If it is pointing to the 6, then it is halfway around the clock face. It shows that it is half past the hour and that there is half an hour to go until the next hour.

When you count round a clock in hours, the sequence is 1, 2, 3, 4, 5, 6, 7, 8, 9, 10, 11, 12. Then, providing you are not working on a 24 hour clock, it all starts again at 1. The same applies to minutes and seconds. When you get to 60 minutes or 60 seconds, you start over again.

This leads to a modification compared to the way you add ordinary numbers when adding seconds, minutes and hours. The modification requires an awareness of the number patterns for time and the appropriate adjustment to these 12, 24 and 60 number patterns. This means we are working with a restricted number of numbers. For example you cannot have a time during the day of 26:45!

Some examples:

40 minutes plus 30 minutes = 70 minutes, which is 60 minutes and 10 minutes, that is 1 hour and 10 minutes.

So 40 min + 30 min = 1 hr 10 min

A 4 hour journey starts at 10 am. What time does it finish?

This can be done as a two stage problem, using 4 as 2 + 2. 10 + 2 takes you to 12 noon. 12 noon + 2 takes you to 2 pm.

So the addition looks like 10 + 4 = 2, which, of course would be nonsense if the numbers were not using the circular 12 base of time.

A flight leaves at 20.00 and lands 8 hours later. What is its arrival time?

20.00 + 8 = 04.00

Again, this can also be done in two stages, going to 24.00 hours first:

20.00 + 4.00 = 24.00, which is also 0.00, then
0.00 + 4.00 = 04.00

If you just looked at the raw additions here, you might think someone was fooling around with maths. In the previous example you could see that 10 add 4 does not normally equal 2. The same is true of this example, 20 plus 8 does not normally equal 4.

For number work with time you have to be very aware of the role of 12, 24 and 60 as 'start again' numbers.

The last example introduced an additional complication for work with time ... the twenty-four hour clock so beloved by train timetablers and travel agents.

There are 24 hours in a day, but, under normal circumstances we work on two circuits of a 12 hour clock and use the letters am and pm to indicate morning or afternoon / evening. So 7 am is a morning time and 7 pm is an evening time. (The first is a breakfast time and the second is a cinema time).

In theory the 24 hour clock should remove any confusion over the time of an aircraft flight or a train time. In theory!

Most people's daily use of time is the 12 hour system, so the 24 hour system is far less familiar. Times such as 15.35 do not trigger the same automatic response and understanding as 3.35 pm.

As a traveller I am almost obsessive about times. I think one of my worse nightmares would be to arrive too late to catch my flight.

So, the translation from 24 hour times to 12 hour times is one I take very carefully, which means I double check (usually twice!)

The translation between the two systems is, of course, two way, 24 hour times to 12 hour times and 12 hour times to 24 hour times. We tend to meet the first translation more often.

Translating 24 hour times to 12 hour times

In a day the hour hand of a clock travels twice around the 12 hour face of the clock. There are 24 hours in a day.

The first 12 hours 59 minutes generate the same numbers for both the 12 hour and 24 hour times since the first circuit of the clock face is the same for 12 and 24 hour times. So 8 am is 08.00 hours,11.00 am is 11.00 hours and 12.45 pm is 12.45 hours.

At 1 pm, the 12 hour time returns to the numbers 1 to 12, but the 24 hour time is now into its second circuit of the clock and 1 pm becomes 1 plus 12 (from the first circuit), that is 13.00. This continues, so 2 pm becomes 2 plus 12, that is 14.00, 3 pm becomes 3 plus12, that is 15.00 and so on.

Consider some comparisons / translations of key times:

12 hour time	24 hour time
12 midnight	00.00
6.00 am	06.00
12 noon	12.00
6.00 pm	18.00

and other examples:

7.30 am	07.30
4.15 pm	16.15
10.30 pm	22.30

The times where mistakes are most likely to occur are the times from 1 pm up to midnight. That is when the two systems become significantly different. So any 24 hour time between 13.00 and 24.00 could cause a problem. For example, a common mistake is to translate 20.00 as 10 pm (when it should be 8 pm).

To convert those 24 hour times which are in the 13.00 to midnight group in to 12 hour times, the first step is to subtract 2 from the 24 hour time to give you the key figure. The second step is to take away 10. All the resulting 12 hour times will be pm.

For example, to translate 19.00 to 12 hour time, first subtract 2:

$$19.00 - 2 = 17.00$$

The 7 will be 7 pm when you have done the second subtraction, which is to take away 10 from 17.00:

$$17.00 - 10 = 7.00 \text{ pm}$$

As double checks, you could:
add back 12 to see if you return to 19.00 or
work back from 24.00 and 12 midnight,
So, compare $24 - 19 = 5$ and $12 - 7 = 5$ or
subtract 12 in one step, $19 - 12 = 7$

Translating 12 hour times to 24 hour times

Again, if you can picture a clock with the hour hand moving round for 24 hours, this should be straightforward. Up to 1.00 pm, the numbers are the same. From 12 noon, the 24 hour time is on its second circuit, but instead of using the 1 to 12 numbers again (in conjunction with pm) the numbers carry on from 12 to be 13, 14, 15, 16, 17, 18, 19, 20, 21, 22, 23 and 24.

To translate the times from 1.00 pm to 12 midnight, simply add 12.

Some examples:

2.40 pm becomes $2.40 + 12 = 14.40$
7.15 pm becomes $7.15 + 12 = 19.15$
10.30 pm becomes $10.30 + 12 = 22.30$

As ever, if you feel more comfortable, do the addition in two steps, either

add 2, then add 10, or
add 10, then add 2.

16 Algebra. Really Scare Your Friends

Quite often when I am talking with teachers about maths learning difficulties I see their eyes glaze over when I mention algebra. Something neurological seems to happen. Algebra triggers a shut down, often accompanied by an obvious attack of anxiety. Sadly, algebra is often viewed as impenetrable and as totally meaningless.

It's a shame that this is so because algebra is so closely related to many maths skills people have already met and, if these early topics have been taught properly, then algebra should be a natural progression.

Algebra can give us ways of writing complicated ideas in a simple way. For example, in Chapter 4, I explained that when we add two numbers it does not matter in which order we add them. For example, adding 8 onto 6 achieves the same answer as adding 6 onto 8 or adding 6 onto 3 gives the same answer as adding 3 onto 6.

I can generalise this rule using algebra. If I use the letter p to represent the first number and the letter s to represent the second number then I can sum up this rule by writing

$$p + s = s + p$$

I can use algebra to write formulas or generalisations in a simple, concise way. For example, the perimeter (the total length of all the sides) of a triangle that has three sides of lengths 3 cm, 4 cm and 5 cm is $3 + 4 + 5 = 12$ cm. The perimeter of a triangle that has three sides of lengths 17 cm, 9 cm and 12 cm is $17 + 9 + 12 = 38$ cm.

I can generalise this into a formula for the perimeter of any triangle. If I generalise the lengths of the three sides by calling them A cm, B cm and C cm then the perimeter, which I write as P, will be represented by a formula

$$P = A + B + C$$

What algebra does for rules and formulas is to generalise by using a letter to represent a number and that letter will then represent any number you have to use with that formula.

Here is another example. If you want to calculate your average speed on a walk you might use the formula,

$$\text{Speed} = \frac{\text{Distance travelled}}{\text{Time taken}}$$

You could write the formula in a shorter form, using letters to represent the three quantities involved, for example, use S for speed, D for distance and T for time. The formula would now look like this

$$S = \frac{D}{T}$$

This formula will enable you to calculate your average speed for any walk, for example if you walked 9 miles in 3 hours, your calculation would start with the formula, but then use the numbers for this particular walk.

$$S = \frac{D}{T} = \frac{9}{3} = 3\text{mph}$$

Some new rules

You have to learn some new conventions and codes in order to read and understand algebra, but after mastering these codes, algebra continues to build on the basic rules you learned for working with numbers. As I have shown above, algebra is useful as a form of generalising. This is a good reason for developing some understanding of this topic.

There are, then, these new conventions attached to algebra, some new codes and rules to be aware of and learn.

For example, algebra does not use a written × sign for multiply. There are probably several reasons for this. I think that one of the reasons is that mathematicians like to present information simply in the sense of as little extra wordage or symbols as possible.

An example of this reduction is the formula for the area of a rectangle (any rectangle). Starting with the word version:

Area of a rectangle = breadth times width = breadth × width

Now use A to represent area and b to represent breadth and w to represent width, so the formula begins to look like algebra

$$A = b \times w$$

But the times sign (×) is not written in algebra:

$$A = bw$$

This formula can be used to give the area of any rectangle. It is a generalisation of the way the areas of all rectangles are calculated. This formula suits mathematicians since it is a very concise way of expressing information. Mathematicians use the word 'elegant' as their top approval rating of a piece of mathematical work. It is most likely that one of the characteristics of an elegant solution is its brevity.

Algebra does not use divide signs either, which is something that you have met with fractions. In fact, fractions are a good example of how algebra represents division.

Fractions and division can be represented in algebra as:

$$\frac{a}{b}$$

This represents any fraction, providing you know that 'a' represents the numerator as any number and that 'b' represents the denominator as any number. This simple generalisation also hides a division sign, as with fractions it means $a \div b$.

Algebra can be a much clearer way of expressing an idea. Look at the next sentence.

I described an idea in the times table chapter which showed that if you multiply two numbers together you get the same answer which ever order you use for the multiplication, for example $4 \times 5 = 20$ and $5 \times 4 = 20$ or $6 \times 3 = 3 \times 6 = 18$.

A much shorter way of saying this in algebra is

$$ps = sp$$

if p is one number and s is another number.

So far we have seen some examples of simple, minimal content equations which put over an idea in a clear way, *providing you know the code*. Of course, all subjects have their own vocabulary and conventions, so algebra is no different in this respect.

Once you know the vocabulary, the code and the conventions of algebra, a complex idea can be communicated clearly. The same is true of many other topics, for example, if a physicist is told something is a 'transverse wave', she can immediately tell you a lot about that wave even before she knows its full identity. If you ask a guitarist to play an 'E chord', that is enough information for him to know where to put his fingers on the six strings of the guitar. If you do not play the guitar, then you do not know the code and E means nothing to you.

Since algebra uses letters to replace some numbers, the letters must behave like numbers and follow the same rules as numbers (and vice versa). This interchange of numbers and letters can help you understand and work out algebra.

For example, in Chapter 4, I explained that multiplication meant adding lots of the same number, such as

$$3 \times 8 = 8 + 8 + 8 \text{ or } 3 \times 7 = 7 + 7 + 7$$

I can generalise this 3x rule for any number, which I represent as 'n', by using the formula

$$3 \times n = 3n = n + n + n$$

I also showed how to group the numbers, which I can show with algebra as,

$$3n = 2n + n$$

If I return to the triangle example from the start of this Chapter, only now I shall make the triangle an equilateral triangle, which is a triangle with three sides all of the same length, and I generalise that each side has a length of A, then the perimeter, P can be worked out from the formula'

$$P = A + A + A$$

And using my knowledge from the multiplication examples above, I can shorten this to:

$$P = 3A$$

Another piece of the code you need to know is for when we do repeated multiplications. A good example of this is working out the volume of a cube.

If a cube has (three equal) sides each of length 5 cm, then we work out the volume by multiplying the three sides together

Volume of the cube = $5 \times 5 \times 5 = 125$ cubic centimetres.

If I generalise this procedure and find the formula for the volume, V, of a cube that has sides, each of length a, then we get

$$V = a \times a \times a$$

The algebra code does not use the times signs, so the equation becomes

$$V = aaa$$

But we write this as

$$V = a^3$$

Which was how we dealt with powers of 10 (see page 75)

If we working out the area of a square, that would have a formula of

$A = a \times a$

$A = aa$ which we write as

$A = a^2$

Making a longer formula

Now, let's make a formula for exchanging pounds into US dollars at a travel agent. This will introduce another item of algebra code, the bracket.

The exchange rate as I write this is $1.96 for £1. The travel agent will take a £4.00 commission fee for doing the exchange.

Start with a number example, say changing £104 into dollars.

Take off the commission £104 − £4 = £100

Now work out how many dollars 100 × 1.96 = $196

This was a two step process:
1) take away the commission
2) multiply the net amount in pounds by the exchange rate for pounds to dollars.

This can now be translated into algebra, using some code letters:
c for commission
p for amount of money in pounds
d for amount of money in dollars
e for exchange rate of £ to $
and brackets ( )

$$d = (p - c)e$$

This looks OK if you know the meaning of the brackets ( ), which are another one of the algebra codes. Some of the codes tell you an instruction, for example + tells you to add. Brackets tell you two linked instructions.

Brackets hold items together, almost like putting them in a box. The brackets around p-c, (p-c), tell you to treat this combination of p and c together.

Brackets also tell you about the priority of using the operations add, subtract, divide and multiply. In building the equation

$$d = (p - c)e$$

we subtracted (step 1) and then multiplied (step 2).

The rule / procedure of an algebra equation like this is DO THE BIT IN THE BRACKET FIRST.

The brackets also mean multiply. In much the same way as the code bw means b multiplied by w, (p-c)e means (p-c) is multiplied by e.

So (p-c)e tells you to

1) do the inside of the bracket first, that is the subtraction p-c

2) multiply the result of this subtraction by e

Which is exactly the procedure we used for the changing the £104 to dollars example.

Algebra equations should always work when you use numbers in place of the letters.

This equation d = (p-c)e would work for any money exchanged with a commission subtracted. You would have to recode the letters, for example to change pounds into Euros the codes would be:

p is amount in pounds (the same as before)

d is the amount in Euros

e is the exchange rate of £ to €.

The quadratic equation (only for the brave)

This is a type of equation that shows you are really beginning to be an algebra star.

$$A = (x + c)(y + b)$$

However complicated that may appear to you, take hope. You have met it before with numbers. Despite its appearance it is only about multiplying together two things at a time. You just have to do that multiplication four times, so

when you multiply the brackets out, the result has four parts

$$A = xy + bx + cy + cb$$

I will try to show you how this is closely linked to the strategies we have used for times table facts and for long multiplication. This should demonstrate once again how the same ideas are recycled (in different disguises) time and again in mathematics.

Let's analyse the equation A = (x + c)(y + b).

It is one number, (x + c) times another number (y + b). For example, remembering that letters represent numbers, x could be 20 and c could be 3, so (x + c) could be 23. In the same way, y could be 40 and b could be 5, making (y + b) as 45. So one example of a number equivalent to

$$(x + c)(y + b)$$

could be 23 × 45

because it is (20 + 3)(40 + 5)

This is a multiplication of two quantities, which is once again the same working out an area.

Now let's set up the area

The area has four sub-areas, so the total area can be calculated by working out the area of the four sub-areas and then adding them together.

Area 1) xy

Area 2) bx

Area 3) cy

Area 4) cb

Total area, $A = xy + bx + cy + cb$

Try this again with another quadratic equation, this time a square.

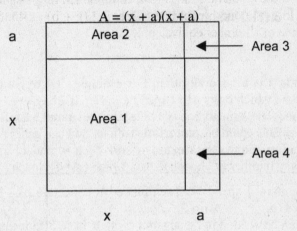

$$A = (x + a)(x + a)$$

Area 1) x^2
Area 2) ax
Area 3) a^2
Area 4) ax

Total area, $A = x^2 + ax + ax + a^2$

The two ax's add together to make $2ax$, so the total area is

$$A = x^2 + 2ax + a^2$$

17 Famous Formulas

A formula is a generalisation. For example, if I buy a bar of chocolate which costs 41p I spend $1 \times 41p$. If I buy two bars of this chocolate I spend $2 \times 41p$ (82p). If I buy three bars, I spend $3 \times 41p$. This could become a little tedious, so I can generalise by using a formula which I can use to work out how much I spend if I buy any number of chocolate bars which cost 41p each.

'The amount I spend' = 'The number of chocolate bars I buy' times '41p'
This can be written in the algebra code. If I use S to mean 'The amount I spend' and n to mean 'The number of chocolate bars I buy'. The formula becomes:

$$S = n \times 41$$

You now have to remember another piece of the code which was mentioned in the Algebra chapter. The convention (normal practice) in maths formulas that use letters to represent the factors involved (in this case S and n) is to not write the times sign (x). This works on the principle that if it's not (written) there you assume it is there!
The formula becomes; $S = 41n$
which is a very short way of writing the formula.

Circles

If there is a scene in a film or play set in a classroom or lecture theatre, especially if it is a science or maths class, then there will be a blackboard and written on it will be

$$A = \Pi r^2.$$

This is the formula for the area of a circle, using r to represent the radius. Π is a special number, a number which is a bit more than 3 and can be written to so many decimal places that this activity can get the successful (and perseverent) person (though really it is their computer) into the Guiness Book of Records.

This special number, which has its own symbol, Π, is called pi. Pi is to do with circles. It is a sort of Glastonbury number. Natural, man.

If you want to try and find an approximate value for pi, take a piece of string and wrap it once around a biggish tin can. This length is called the circumference. Measure it. Now, as accurately as you can, measure the diameter of the can

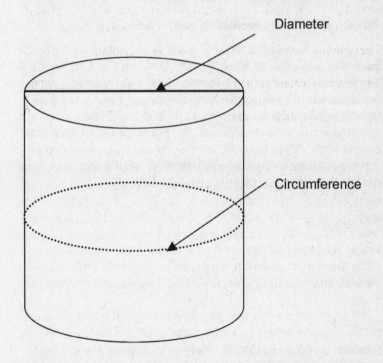

Diameter

Circumference

Divide the circumference by the diameter and the result should be an approximate value for pi. A reasonably accurate value is 3.147.

Pi is the ratio of the circumference of a circle to its diameter, that is the circumference of a circle divided by its diameter.

$$\Pi = \frac{C}{d}$$

You can turn this formula around to

$$C = \Pi d$$

so you can calculate the circumference of any circle if you know its diameter.

Pi also features in the formula for the area of a circle, as I said in the opening paragraph of this chapter.

$$\text{Area of a circle} = \Pi r^2$$

For some people the word formula is an immediate barrier. I think this is another example of the vocabulary of maths adding a mystique that keeps some learners away. This use of a special vocabulary is not unique to maths. You can find it in many places, for example, computer users speak of RAM and ROM, language specialists talk about graphemes and phonemes, car experts talk about torque. If you have the motivation and if someone explains these words without using even more specialist words in their explanation, then you can understand what they mean.

Pythagoras

The Pythagoras equation (or formula) is sufficiently famous for it to be the subject of a rather long and somewhat contrived joke, which I am not telling here, involving a squaw and a hippopotamus.

Pythagoras was a Greek who lived about 2500 years ago. He set up a secret religious society that explored the mysteries of number. He believed that the study of arithmetic was the way to perfection (something governments seem to believe when discussing numeracy).

Pythagoras was not the first to discover the theorem that now bears his name. The Chinese used it for surveying and the

Egyptians used it to help build the pyramids. This famous theory has enabled builders to produce set squares of exactly 90°. It has to be a pretty useful equation.

For a nation of such great architects as the ancient Greeks, an accurate measure of 90° would have been essential. A consequence of the Pythagoras theory was a special case of a right angled triangle, the 3, 4, 5 triangle. This is a triangle whose three sides are 3 units, 4 units and 5 units. If these sides are measured accurately and joined accurately, the resulting triangle includes an exact right angle.

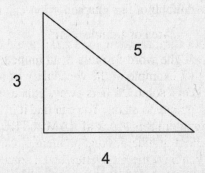

Pythagoras's equation deals with the lengths of the three sides of any right angle triangle. If you square the lengths of the two smaller sides and add those two squares together then that gives the same number as the square of the length of the longest side. (This longest side, opposite the right angle, is called the hypotenuse).

$$a^2 + b^2 = c^2$$

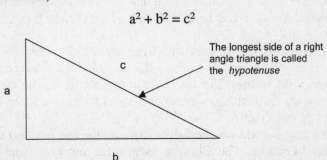

The longest side of a right angle triangle is called the *hypotenuse*

In the 3, 4, 5 triangle, the shorter sides are, obviously, 3 and 4.

The square of 3 is 3×3 $3 \times 3 = 9$
The square of 4 is 4×4 $4 \times 4 = 16$
The sum of these two squares is $9 + 16 = 25$.

The square of 5 is 5×5 $5 \times 5 = 25$.

For the practical construction of a right angle, this 3, 4, 5 triangle is the simplest example of Pythagoras's equation. It is possible to have multiples of 3, 4 and 5 such as 6, 8 and 10 (where all three sides have been doubled as in all proportion calculations, see Chapter 12).

The next whole number example of this special equation is a little less practical. The three sides are 5, 12 and 13.

The two short sides are 5 and 12.
The square of 5 is 5×5 $5 \times 5 \ = \ 25$
The square of 12 is 12×12 $12 \times 12 = 144$
The sum of the two squares is $\overline{25 + 14 = 169}$
The longest side is 13.
The square of the longest side (the hypotenuse) is 13×13
$13 \times 13 = 169$.

It is fascinating to think that these calculations are thousands of years old. Number facts endure!

18 Dyscalculia

Dyscalculia means a problem in doing any maths.

Dyscalculia is sometimes understood to be like dyslexia but with numbers instead of words. We do not yet have the same knowledge about dyscalculia that we have about dyslexia, but research is being carried out, most notably by Professor Brian Butterworth at University College, London.

It seems likely that some peoples' brains are not efficiently 'wired' for maths. This may well be a side issue of Howard Gardner's theory of multiple intelligences. What Gardner says is that there are several intelligences, for example, a mathematical intelligence, a music intelligence or an art intelligence. Quite understandably, we do not all have these intelligences in equal measures. It could be that our mathematical intelligence is not our best intelligence!

Dyscalculia is used to describe someone who has severe difficulties with maths. Of course, we have to think about what we mean by 'severe'. A survey carried out in 2006 in the UK suggested that half of the working population cannot do maths beyond the level taught to 11 year old pupils in schools. However, it would be unlikely that 50% of our population is dyscalculic.

I wrote some answers to FAQ's from teachers for a DfES website. Here is my answer to the question, 'How do I recognise a child who has dyscalculia?'

'As a basic indicator, the child will be performing below expectations (primarily yours, the teacher's) with no obvious reason such as emotional state or an illness such as, say, glandular fever. This underachievement may manifest itself in specifics such as problems with knowing the value or worth of numbers, for example in not realising that 9 is one less than 10, or being able to rapidly recall (as the National Numeracy Strategy requires) basic number facts, or perhaps a totally mechanical application of procedures with no understanding of why or what the result means or how to evaluate the answer.'

I do think that this unfortunately high percentage is partly a consequence of the way that maths is often taught as just a collection of rules and facts to remember and not necessarily to understand. If we do not practise maths that we know and the maths that we do know is based purely on memory, then we will forget the maths.

Understanding maths is a much more robust outcome than just trying to remember maths.

This seems to me to be the reason why we may have many more dyscalculics and weak mathematicians in the adult population than in the school population.

I have tried to show different ways of approaching maths in Dealing with Dyscalculia which reduce the number of facts you need to memorise and which link together many of the processes you need to manipulate numbers.

I have set up 31 questions to help you think about your own abilities in maths. If you tick more than half of these questions, then you may need to consider being checked out for dyscalculia.

Checklist for Dyscalculia

Do you
1) Have difficulty remembering addition facts ☐
2) Have difficulty counting objects accurately. ☐
3) Lack the ability to make 'one to one correspondence' when counting (match the number to the object) ☐
4) Find it impossible to 'see' that four objects are 4 without counting (or 3, if a young child) ☐
5) Count on for addition facts, as for 7 + 3, counting on 8,9, 10 to get your answer ☐

6) Count all the numbers when adding, as for 7 + 3 again, you count 1,2,3,4,5,6,7,8,9,10 (which would be a stronger indicator of dyscalculia than Q5) ☐

7) Use tally marks for addition or subtraction problems ☐

8) Find it much harder to count backwards compared to forwards ☐

9) Find it difficult to count fluently less familiar sequences, such as: 1,3,5,7,9,11 … or 14,24,34,44, 54,64 … ☐

10) Only know the 2x, 5x and 10 multiplication facts. ☐

11) Count on to access the 2x and 5x facts ☐

12) Remember being able to learn the other multiplication facts, but then forget them overnight ☐

13) Make 'big' errors for multiplication facts, such as $6 \times 7 = 67$ or $6 \times 7 = 13$ ☐

14) Find it difficult to write numbers which have zeros within them, such as, 'three hundred and four' or 'four thousand and twenty one' ☐

15) Find it difficult to judge whether an answer is right, or nearly right ☐

16) Find estimating impossible. ☐

17) Struggle with mental arithmetic. ☐

18) Forget the question asked in mental arithmetic ☐

19) Like to use formulas (when you remember them!), but use them mechanically without any understanding of how they work ☐

20) Forget mathematical procedures, especially as they become more complex, such as decomposing or borrowing for subtraction and almost certainly any method for division. ☐

21) Find it difficult to progress from the materials (counters, blocks, tallies) to the numbers ☐

22) Think that algebra is impossible to understand ☐

23) Organise your written work poorly, for example you do not line up columns of numbers properly. ☐

24) Have poor skills with money, for example, are you unable to calculate change from a purchase. ☐

25) 'See' numbers literally and not inter-related, for example, do you count from 1 to get 9, rather than subtracting 1 away from 10. □

26) Think an item priced at £4.99 is '£4 and a bit' rather than almost £5 □

27) Get very anxious about doing ANY maths □

28) Refuse to try any maths, especially unfamiliar topics. □

29) Not see and pick up patterns or generalisations, especially ones that are new to you, for example that $\frac{1}{2}, \frac{1}{3}, \frac{1}{4}, \frac{1}{5}$ is a sequence that is getting smaller. □

30) Not 'see' immediately that $7 + 5$ is the same as $5 + 7$ or that 7×3 is the same as 3×7. □

31) Become impulsive when doing maths, rather than being analytical. Do you rush to get it over with? □

19 People Having Difficulty with Maths

There are many reasons why people fail to do well in mathematics. Usually there are ways to overcome or at least lessen their problems. Obviously not everyone is going to achieve or want to achieve a degree in maths but mostly we should all be able to find a level of success that should meet our needs.

In this chapter I have described the problems of three learners to illustrate where the problem begins. Perhaps there are some similarities to difficulties you have experienced. I have also included the reactions of Ann, a successful career woman who was suddenly faced with a mathematics module in her studies for a Masters degree ... a classic case of mathematics anxiety. Let's begin with Ann

Ann

Ann is a 56 year old grandmother, with a degree in social studies and a very successful career, who decided to take a Masters degree. Two year's into the course Ann discovered she had to take a statistics module. She wrote to me for advice. She told me that at school she had been removed from maths classes at age 12 years for being unteachable in this subject!

I sent her the WRAT screening test, a basic maths test which allows a maximum of 15 minutes for your efforts. The WRAT, is the Wide Range Achievement Test which is an American screening test for basic skills. I provided Ann with the maths part of the test.

This is an extract from the letter she sent back with the test, perhaps the most moving letter I have ever received about difficulties with maths …

Dear Steve,

Thank you for sending the WRAT (the Wide Range Achievement Test) test. The few I managed to do in 15 minutes (I could not have done any more of the test even if you had given me 15 hours!) did not surprise me (even with the help of pen and paper). What did surprise me was the overwhelming sense of panic and deep sadness I felt as I tried to do it.

I sat at my own dining room table, no noise, no pressure and I felt like I was 10 years old again. I still feel shaken by my emotional response to this little test, I just felt I had to write to you straight away before the feelings fade. I just know that if I had been a 10 year old boy doing the test while someone waited in the room, I would have torn it into pieces and run out of the room; I would have wanted to hit anyone who tried to stop me.

As it was I was taken right back to my parents' dining room table 46 years ago when I was 10 years old, trying so hard to understand the homework to prepare me for the 11+ examinations. As I sat there as a 56 year old mother, grandmother, qualified social worker, etc, the intense emotional response was overwhelming. I felt myself fighting back the tears, my hands starting to shake, my whole body tense. I just wanted to put my head down into my hands and sob. I found myself saying 'I can't do it'. I felt an overwhelming sense of failure and despair.

I am writing this, not for sympathy, but because I am grateful to have gained an insight that I could not have otherwise achieved …

On a personal level, I feel quite proud of what I have achieved despite my learning deficit in respect of numbers. It may just be possible that I have achieved more because of the anger generated by feeling such a failure. Who knows. It really is not important for me anymore. I suddenly feel that by chasing academic achievement all these years I have been trying to compensate for feeling stupid. ('If I get A levels I can't be stupid; if I get a BA I can't be stupid; if I get an MA I can't be stupid, etc') …

Ann's letter illustrates how the consequences of being unsuccessful in maths can affect many aspects of your life. Whilst Ann was spurred on, trying to compensate for this area of failure, others may just give in and confine themselves to the safe options in life.

Whilst researching aspects of mathematics for this book I carried out informal assessments (that is assessments which did not consist of just standard tests) on several children who were having difficulties with maths. They were all very much individuals in their problems. There was, however, a common factor, a failure to learn all the times table facts.

I chose the word 'failure' in the last sentence very deliberately, because that is what it seemed to each of the children. One day, it will be understood that there are a number of children who, despite their very best efforts, cannot learn all the times table facts. I am not saying that children should not try, but I am saying that parents and/or teachers who persist in insisting that they do try, risk demotivating the child. Do not set a target that is out of reach of the child.

In any assessment of maths I rely heavily on simple questions rather than any deeply significant and complex psychological question. My favourite is "How did you do that?' Sometimes I rephrase it as say, 'Can you tell me how you worked that out?' and sometimes, 'Can you think of another way to do that?' but it's a good strategy, especially if the person cannot guess what answer they think you want to hear. It certainly deals with any preconceived ideas I may be about to attribute to the person doing the work.

For example, I was working with a 15year old boy who was doing quite well in maths (he achieved a grade B in GCSE maths). I discovered that he calculated 3×6 by halving the answer to 6×6. 'Aha' I say, leaping to a sweeping generalisation, 'I have noticed that many people who cannot remember all the times table facts, do know the square number facts.' James put me right. 'I know just the 6×6 fact because when I lost my two front teeth as a child, my speech therapist made me say six times six is thirty six over and over again.'

Lorna

Lorna, aged 12 came to see me after her educational psychologist suggested her parents might like to seek a little more information on her maths difficulties. He had found her achievements in maths to be around 3 years behind expectations. Lorna's IQ was at the lower end of average, but she had good language skills. Her psychologist described her as having, 'little faith in her own ability in maths, possibly comparing this unfavourably to her good skills in language.'

Lorna certainly had lost faith in herself and, understandably, took a little while to involve herself in the maths tasks I asked her to do. (The best way to learn about someone's maths abilities is to watch them doing some maths, preferably encouraging them to talk you through their procedures and thoughts).

Lorna had good counting skills that were both accurate and quick. She did most of the counting in her head (some children use dots or tallies to keep track, others may finger count). For 9 + 8 she added, by counting in her head, first 5, and then 3. She also answered quickly and accurately, using the same procedure, 9 + 6 (added 3 and 3) and 9 + 4 (added 2 and 2).

Although she used the same strategy again for ? + 8 = 14 and 9 + ? = 13, this different, slightly less familiar presentation was answered more slowly.

Lorna said she could do most times tables, but 'didn't know the 9's.' In reality, she did not have immediate recall of these facts. She counted on. She was good at this, and was, for example, able to count on in 3's and 7's. I asked her 'What are eight nines?'. Lorna said she didn't know the nine times table (she had told me this earlier). I asked her if she could tell me the answer to nine eights, which she did by counting on in eights. Lorna could count backwards accurately.

Lorna was also able to adapt the familiar sequence 10, 20, 30, 40 ... to a less familiar form; 12, 22, 32, 42 ...

It was interesting to see someone who was so adept at sequencing with quite difficult numbers. She was able to adapt patterns, but Lorna obviously was not aware that 8×9 and 9×8

gave the same answer and she had not absorbed the pattern of adding 9, which is easier than the pattern of adding 8. I find similar examples of anomalies in skills in many people. It would be dangerous to make assumptions along the lines of, 'If they can do A then they can do B.'

It is possible to extend the existing skills such people have into new areas, because the groundwork is there. It is about knowing what groundwork is there and then building on it in a way that is accessible to and empathetic to the learner.

Another example of an apparently inconsistent skill was in naming numbers that contained zeros, for example she named 9026 as nine hundred and twenty six, but named 1205 as twelve hundred and five (easier to say than ninety hundred and twenty six). She had little understanding of zero. This is a not uncommon disparity for many people.

Lorna is an inchworm (see Chapter 1). She also rushes her work and an inchworm who combines impulsivity with a poor knowledge of basic facts and procedures is in some mathematical danger!

If Lorna is not encouraged to develop her existing effective counting skills into more sophisticated maths skills her progress will be limited. The problem with moving someone away from an inefficient, but secure skill is that they are likely to resist and, when they do try, will probably do less well until the new skill is mastered.

Unfortunately, Lorna had no concept of money. This is unfortunate on two counts. One is that money is a good teaching aid, and two is that knowing about money is a life skill.

This gap in her knowledge showed up in her answers to two decimal questions. Lorna interpreted 12.3 + 5 as 12 + 3 + 5 and 63 + 2.1 as 63 + 2 + 1. Money is a good teaching aid for decimals, but only if you understand money!

There are certain priority targets to aim at if Lorna is to progress. I spoke of the maths wall being able to stand with some bricks missing (page 4). Lorna's maths wall needs some more bricks before it can support its present state and certainly before it can be built any higher. As ever, she has to be taught to build on what she knows and to be taught in the way that is sympathetic to the way she works (her inchworm cognitive style).

Jill

Jill was a fascinating example of a person with a specific difficulty in mathematics. She came to see me with her Mum, who gave me an impressive pen picture of her daughter.

Jill was 14 years old. She was in the gifted group at her comprehensive school. Jill taught herself to read when she was three and now reads around twenty books a week. At fourteen she was teaching herself Hebrew and Sanscript. She arrived in my office with a copy of Virgil, in Latin of course (which, without question was the subject which gave me my most catastrophic failures at school).

Jill's Mum felt that Jill's early lessons in maths were inappropriate. Also Jill did not get the same positive feedback she received from her work in English and foreign languages.

Despite being in the gifted group at school, Jill was in the middle set for maths. Not surprisingly, when you think of the nature of the sciences, she liked biology more, and did better in it, than in chemistry and physics.

Initially, Jill avoided answering any open ended questions, but as she became less threatened by the conversations she provided some clear observations of her own strengths and weaknesses in maths. She summed up her problems in maths as, ' I think I understand it, I write it down, but then I've missed something vital. Suddenly I can't remember things.' (This last statement from someone who can obviously remember several languages. Jill is an example of an individual with the specific memory blocks that seem to be related to maths and could well classify as a dyscalculic).

I scattered some poker chips on the table and asked her to estimate how many were there. She protected herself by saying 'It's a wild guess' and guessed 35. She accurately counted the 51 chips, without grouping them in tens or fives, which would have allowed her to check the answer.

I like the task where I give ten one pence coins, five two pence coins and two five pence coins and ask the person to show me as many ways as they can to make 9p, using the coins as many times as they wish. Jill showed that her sense of number values, even at this level, was poor and that she did not tackle this task logically.

On the WRAT Test, this gifted girl scored at the 23rd percentile, that is 77% of her age group would do better.

I asked Jill to give me an easier number, an estimate, for 882 (one of the numbers from a question on the WRAT test). She suggested 880. Taken with other observations, it seems that Jill has poor, or at least rather cautious, estimation skills and a poor concept of relations in numbers and possibly the concept of an 'easy' number, in this case 900. This deficit in estimation skills does not support her grasshopper thinking style.

I feel that an inclination towards a particular thinking style is inherent, but the back up skills you need to be successful with that style often need to be learned (and therefore taught).

Jill needs to develop a sense of the values of numbers to enable her to maximise the potential value of her grasshopper style. This feeling about Jill was further supported by her answers to some questions that two colleagues from the USA and I designed to investigate thinking style. One of my favourite questions for this is a chess board like square of 49 black and white little squares. The question is, 'How many of the squares are black?' The answer is 25 (and thus 24 are white). Inchworms often count the squares to get their answer, but grasshoppers just look at the picture and say '25 black'. Jill looked at the picture and said, 'It's either 24 or 25, I just can't make up my mind which.' She had that holistic ability to look and almost see an answer, but didn't quite have enough number skills to be sure of her answer.

Jill used strategies to compensate for her poor ability to recall basic facts. For example she derived $9 + 8$ from $9 + 9 - 1$ and $9 + 6$ from $10 + 6 - 1$. She computed 8×5 from half of 8×10. This suggests that inchworm skills are not her natural inclination. Further support for this was her reluctance to write down any 'working.'

Jill had developed a fatalistic vagueness in her attitude to maths. I particularly liked her explanation of her error with

$$\begin{array}{r} 391 \\ -\ 88 \\ \hline 317 \end{array}$$

Jill looked at the units column, where she had, incorrectly, taken 1 from 8 and said, 'I take away the number which is more convenient without realising it.'

There is no doubt that Jill should be taught, as indeed should anyone, by methods which acknowledge her abilities, thinking style and her weaknesses. She will not survive the sausage factory approach, where one of the (misguided) principles is 'Do it this way.'

Harry

Harry was 12 years 7 months when his father asked me to look at his work in maths. The father was concerned about the level of Harry's maths performance as he approached common entrance examinations. Harry was in the upper sets for all subjects except maths and science.

Harry worked cheerfully and cooperatively throughout the assesment. (I am often amazed by how perseverant some children are despite the less than positive experience they have of maths).

He showed some of the anomalies I have come to expect when I ask children to work through some maths questions. For example, Harry used subtraction procedures accurately, except when a zero was involved.

There seems to be a widespread problem with understanding zero, particularly in subtractions. It could be that the idea of taking something away from nothing is just too far outside a child's perception of fairness to be a comfortable action.

Harry was able to convert $\frac{3}{4}$ to 75% and $\frac{3}{8}$ to 37.5% (perhaps he saw the link). He could work out 20% of 120, but incorrectly converted $52\frac{1}{2}$% to 52.5. He avoided the fraction questions.

Harry had quick recall of basic addition and subtraction facts to 20. He used strategies for some addition facts, for example, 7 + 8 was quickly calculated via 7 + 7. He did 9 + 8 was done via 10 + 8 and 14 − 8 was done in two steps as 14 − 4 = 10 and 10 − 4 = 6.

I asked Harry which times table facts he knew. He said he knew the times table facts, 'OK, though I may not know them straight away.' When I asked which ones he did know straight away, Harry said the 2×, 5× and 10×. However, he knows and uses the commutative property (this is the transposal of numbers, for example, 3×4 to 4×3, which still gives the same answer, in this case, 12). He answered 3×8 via 2×8 plus 4 and 4. 6×9 was done via 6×10 minus 6 and 7×6 was done as 6×6 plus 6.

He used quite sophisticated strategies. During this part of our session Harry said, 'I'm good at working things out in my mind, it's showing my working out that's the problem.'

Harry showed distinctly grasshopper tendencies with the cognitive style questions I asked him to try. I looked at his exercise book from school. There was little doubt that Harry's teacher was an inchworm and that he expected Harry to use those methods. One of the reasons a pupil may fail to learn in school is a mismatch in thinking style.

Harry does not like formulas and does not see any reason to use them. Sadly the reality of life in many schools is still that the pupils have to survive an inflexible regime of school maths and will need to learn how to use formulas, even if this is not their preferred way of doing maths. It will actually be of benefit to a pupil like Harry to learn some of the characteristics of the inchworm thinking style, but he will need to be convinced of the benefits. At the moment, he has alternate ways of arriving at answers that are easy for him. He sees no reason to change to procedures that he thinks are longer and more cumbersome than his own.

Harry also needed to improve his skills with word problems.

One of the ways to help this skill is to teach children to take a number equation (like $12 + 5 = 17$) and for them to make up their own word problem around these numbers. Initially, children tend to be very stilted (I have 12 pens, you have 5 pens. How many pens do we have altogether?). They can be led to far more creative and devious stories! In learning how to construct stories, they learn how to deconstruct them too.

Harry has all the basic abilities for success in maths. Like so many children he has not organised his skills to maximise their potential, nor has he recognised all the patterns and inter-relationships in maths. Although he does extend facts he could be taught to be even more creative and effective with this ability. A potential problem is his extreme reliance on a grasshopper style and this is preventing him from tackling formulas and could also cause a breakdown in communication between teacher and child. Sadly it is often the reality that the child is expected to do all the adapting!

Appendix 1

Two words from the maths vocabulary used in this book

I have used the words digit and number quite specifically to mean:

Digit. Any of the symbols, 0, 1, 2, 3, 4, 5, 6, 7, 8, 9

Number. Any of the digits, used individually or combined to represent a value. For example, 14 is fourteen, 506 is five hundred and six. (See also place value in Chapter 2).

Appendix 2

The Inchworm and Grasshopper Test

Try these questions and remember how you worked out the answers. Do questions 1, 2 and 3 in your head. You can use paper and pen/pencil for questions 4 and 5.

1. $432 + 96$

2. $621 - 198$

3. $2 \times 3 \times 4 \times 5$

4. Red pens cost 17p and blue pens cost 13p. If I buy two red pens and two blue pens how much do I pay?

5.

How many squares have a $\heartsuit$?

How did you do the questions?

Q1. Inchworm method
If you visualised, in your head, the numbers rewritten as

$$432$$
$$+96$$

and you added them, starting with the 2 and the 6, making 8
then the 3 and the 9, making 12
you 'carry' the 1 from 12 and add the 1 and the 4, making 5
You reverse the order in which you computed these numbers to
get an answer of 528.
If you used this method or a method that was very similar, give
yourself an I (for Inchworm).

Q1. Grasshopper method
If you looked at the 96 and rounded it up to 100 by adding on 4
Then added 100 to 432 to get 532
Then subtracted the added on 4 to get 528
Give yourself a G for Grasshopper.

Q2. Inchworm method
If you visualised, in your head, the numbers rewritten as

$$621$$
$$-198$$

and then you used a set method, such as 'decomposing' or 'borrowing'

$$
\begin{array}{ccc}
5 & 11 & 1 \\
\cancel{6} & \cancel{2} & 1 \\
-1 & 9 & 8 \\
\hline
4 & 2 & 3 \\
\end{array}
$$

or equal additions

$$
\begin{array}{ccc}
 & & 1 \\
6 & 2 & 1 \\
2 & 0 & \\
\underline{-1} & \underline{9} & \underline{8} \\
4 & 2 & 3
\end{array}
$$

or any formula/set procedure (the sort you would normally write on paper), give yourself an I for Inchworm

Q2. Grasshopper method.
If you looked at the 198 and rounded it up to 200 by adding on 2
Then subtracted 200 from 621 to get 421
Then added on 2, because subtracting 198 instead of 200 gives you an answer that is 2 more, to get 423
If you used this method, give yourself a G for Grasshopper.

Q3. Inchworm method
You will calculate your answer in the order that the numbers are presented in the question,
so you will start with $2 \times 4 = 8$
then $8 \times 3 = 24$
then $24 \times 5 = 120$
If you used (or attempted) this method then give yourself an I for Inchworm.

Q3. Grasshopper method
You will have scanned over all the numbers and spotted a $2 \times$ and a 5. You will start with this easy fact and obtain 10.
$2 \times 5 = 10$
Then you will multiply $4 \times 3 = 12$
Then $12 \times 10 = 120$
If you used this method or something very similar, give yourself a G for Grasshopper.

Q4. Inchworm method
If you do the question in the order that it is written, that is you

work out the cost of two red pens first
either by adding 17 + 17 or by 2 × 17 to get 34p
then you work out the cost of two blue pens
either by adding 13 + 13 or by 2 × 13 to get 26p
then you add 34 and 26 to get 60p
You have taken the question literally, that is you have let the order in which the question presents the information dictate the method.
If you used this method or something very similar give, yourself an I for Inchworm.

Q4. Grasshopper method
You will have read the question through. You will have seen the 7 and the 3 from the 17 and 13 and realised that they add to make 10.
So you will add 17 and 13 to make 30p and then double this to achieve 60p.
You have looked for easy number combinations to help you make the calculations easier.
If you used this method or something very similar, give yourself a G for Grasshopper.

Q5. Inchworm method
If you counted all the squares with a ♡ around the figure to get 15 squares with a ♡ then give yourself an I for Inchworm.
If you added the 5 ♡ across the top, the 5 ♡ across the bottom and the 2 ♡ on the left side to the 3 ♡ on the right side (sometimes people count in the corner ♡ twice)
Then give yourself an I for Inchworm.

Q5. Grasshopper method
If you looked at the whole figure and saw the pattern of 9 squares in the middle that do not have an ♡, plus the one square on the left side without an ♡, you 'see' 10 squares without an ♡ and subtract this from 25 to get 15 squares with an ♡.
If you used this method, give yourself a G for Grasshopper.

Which thinking style are you?

Now you can count up your I and G methods. In an ideal world you would be able to use both methods appropriately, so a mix of I and G methods would be good. If, however you have collected 5 G or 5 I methods then you are at the less flexible end of 'harmonious' thinking styles and the methods by which you learn best may well be defined by your thinking style.

However, there are as ever, some cautions:

1. You may have adopted an inchworm style because that was the way you were taught.
2. You may use both styles in the same question, perhaps using a grasshopper method to get a first answer and then checking it with an inchworm method.
3. You may be an inchworm with number problems, but a grasshopper with other types of question (such as Q5) or vice versa.

Having access to both thinking styles helps you to check any answer and provides that comforting secure feeling about your answer.